THE BACK HOME SERIES

SERIES TITLES

The Arc of the Escarpment
Robert Root

Soul of the Outdoors
Dave Greschner

From the Heart: The Story of Matrix
John Harmon

The Long Fields
Anne-Marie Oomen

Kick Out the Bottom
Erik Mortenson & Christopher Kramer

Wrong Tree: Adventures in Wildlife Biology
Jeff Wilson

At the Lake
Jim Landwehr

Body Talk
Takwa Gordon

The In-Between State
Martha Lundin

North Freedom
Carolyn Dallmann

Ohio Apertures
Robert Miltner

Our Bodies Are Mostly Water

a memoir

Katherine Riegel

CORNERSTONE PRESS
UNIVERSITY OF WISCONSIN-STEVENS POINT

Cornerstone Press, Stevens Point, Wisconsin 54481
Copyright © 2025 Katherine Riegel
www.uwsp.edu/cornerstone

Printed in the United States of America by
Point Print and Design Studio, Stevens Point, Wisconsin

Library of Congress Control Number: 2025934437
ISBN: 978-1-960329-90-5

This is a work of nonfiction. All of the events in this book are true to the best of
the author's memories. Some names and identifying features have been changed to
protect the identity of certain parties. The author in no way represents any company,
corporation, or brand, mentioned herein. The views expressed in this book are solely
those of the author.

Cornerstone Press titles are produced in courses and internships offered by the
Department of English at the University of Wisconsin–Stevens Point.

DIRECTOR & PUBLISHER
Dr. Ross K. Tangedal

EXECUTIVE EDITORS
Jeff Snowbarger, Freesia McKee

EDITORIAL DIRECTOR
Brett Hill

SENIOR EDITOR
Ellie Atkinson

PRESS STAFF
Paige Biever, Karlie Harpold, Lillian Kulbeck, Allison Lange, Sophie McPherson,
Ava Willett, Madison Schultz, Autumn Vine

for my sister, Dorey

ALSO BY KATHERINE RIEGEL:

Love Songs from the End of the World

What the Mouth Was Made For

Castaway

Letters to Colin Firth

CONTENTS

I

II

III

IV

V

We are imperfect mortal beings . . . so wired that when we mourn our losses we also mourn, for better or for worse, ourselves.

—Joan Didion, from *The Year of Magical Thinking*

Dear night skies of the 1970s, dear open barn door, dear hay forts and hawthorn trees blooming as extravagantly as you thorned, dear shared bedroom, twin beds with blue spreads printed calico, dear calico cat catching mice in the barn, dear horse smell on our clothes, dear last night I slept there, dear books read aloud, dear 23rd psalm on the wall above my bed, dear sun tea with lemon, dear diet bars my brother and I stole because they looked like they were covered in chocolate, dear dirt I put in my mouth to see what it tasted like, dear strands of spiderweb in the rafters, dear rides across harvested cornfields, dear dark mornings before school when we pounded ice out of the water buckets, dear dinner table dramas trying not to anger my father, dear brother's spilled milk, dear sister standing up from the table, dear shaggy dog jokes, dear animal-shaped placemats, dear quiet, dear chasing the dog across snowy fields before he found the neighbor's chickens again, dear dirt clod fights between brothers, dear now dead mother, dear now dead father, dear now dead sister, dear three of us left, it will take everything, all of you, to carry me to my own inevitable ending, unforgetting, vivid, your light going out across the universe forever and ever, amen.

Dear Sister,

Our niece's baby is due March 5th. I thought you should know, so you could influence the heavens to bring her March 4th, your birthday—or March Forth, the martial date, as my friend C would say, her students groaning at the pun. I say *her* for our great-niece, but they have decided not to find out the baby's sex. Maybe with each generation it will matter less, pre-determined gender roles as obsolete as rotary phones, too awkward and inefficient to use anymore.

I never thought I would have to do this without you. I expected to look on, over your shoulder, as you held our brothers' squirming descendants and crooned the wordless songs you carried in your chest, the songs you wanted to give your own progeny. My job was to comfort you in your childlessness, to make fun of myself and my choices so everyone would laugh at the relative who claimed dogs were better than kids because they napped when I did and I could leave them home by themselves. Remember when that five-year-old niece pretended to be a dog, crawling under the table and barking in response to questions? But it was you who pulled her onto your lap, tickling her until she giggled as her girl-self. You even showed me how to love my own stepdaughter, the redhead I met as a teen who baffled me with her extroversion.

You are the ghost I bring to every family event. I feel you like a lost leg. The paradox: how what's missing can hurt so much. I want to sew a life-sized doll of you to bring with me so I am recognizable as merely half of a pair of sisters. Even our brothers seem to look for you beside me, their eyes focusing on an outline their memories insist should be visible. At the last wedding I offered condolences to the wrong in-law's in-law, because you were not there to help me sort out who was who, to say the right thing because you always *saw* people, taking them in with your blue eyes, mapping human connections.

Two weeks ago the temperatures here plummeted to the single digits, and already the bluebirds are scouting nesting boxes. New life is supposed to save the world, but with so much spinning away each second, I'm not sure how. Maybe it's a new world every morning, having rebuilt itself from the atom up in the darkness. Maybe all the babies have to do is save the world *today*.

Love,

Your little sister, who you called *Babycakes*, then fell down on the softball field laughing

Mermaid

My sister and I both favored fantasy when it came to reading for fun. Stories where people spoke with trees, breathed underwater, held magic between their palms. Worlds that were green, not smothered under concrete, where the dark was stars and moon and faerie light. Tales where feelings mattered more than money, where relationships guided life and love was simple. Deep psychology, Jungian, darkness and light.

So this is her story:

She was a mermaid in the womb, as all first daughters of her people, though by the time she was born she had two legs and two arms like the rest of humankind. But she never forgot the feeling of being at home in water, and every chance she had she immersed herself. The sea was her favorite, the salt buoying her, the dolphins flicking their tails at her in recognition.

In her childhood she sang songs when she woke in the morning, and again as she went to bed at night—songs about the day she would have and the day that unfolded and how much she loved her mother and her father and her pets, and eventually her little siblings. Horses loved her and carried her willingly, arching their necks and stepping carefully as she asked. In the springtime she picked flowers to weave in their manes and slept in the barn to welcome their foals.

When she was sixteen, she was riding a horse over jumps and he fell, rolling on top of her. She was asleep for seven days and when she awoke she was different, the trajectory of her life changed. It would be harder after that, some of her magic gone, and where before she learned and knew things like plucking dandelion seeds out of the air, afterwards she struggled. She still sang, once so sweetly that her grandmother would awake near her death and think she was already in heaven with the angels. But behind her eyes darkness ebbed and flowed, a sadness she could not control.

Eventually she left home and went out into the world, naïve, one part of her heart still with the horses and the house in the country that were sold just before she left so she lost her whole childhood in one sad summer. She could never go home again. Somehow the water always bubbled up through her anyway, she could make anyone giggle along with her when the mood struck, a silver magic very much like a child's.

Love poured from her like water, too, a presence that soothed and held people in need. Decades came and went, and she slipped through jobs and cities like they were nets meant to catch her, but in every place she found ways to give solace and help and grace. She desperately wanted a little mermaid-child of her own, swimming in her own body, but her love stories were too complex, the boys and men creatures of the hard bones of the world who could not give enough.

Her last home had horses again, finally. She spoke to them and they to her, their voices rich as the earth where she had grown up. There was a man, a love, but his anger rode him like a scorpion, and when she wasn't afraid, she was angry, and when she wasn't angry, she was sad. Still the love poured out of her boundless heart, the heart of water as big as the ocean.

She sang until she could not sing anymore, her body slowly turning back to its mermaid self, abandoning the air. When her friends and family came at the end they didn't understand, they looked on her and saw she was struggling to breathe. Finally she gave herself over, rising up and sinking down to the water again all at once. She returned to magic as she had come from it.

And when she was gone, her friends and family and all the people of the land knew she was the last of her kind, and they cried their love for her loudly, and hoped wherever she went she would be able to hear them.

And I, her sister, who only ever wanted her to be happy, heard her singing thereafter in every dewdrop and still pool, every clear stream and green pond, every brave waterfall and foamy wave.

If I Never Had Anything Good, I Wouldn't Mourn It

Every morning I wake to music in my head. Today it is *Oh Danny boy, the pipes the pipes are calling*, and the birds fall and rise from the grass under the feeder, a flock of diminutive pine siskins punctuated by cardinals. My family sang, not for performance but for joy—rounds at home and in the barn, the melody hard to hold if I was the only one on my strand, and folk songs and even hymns. Carols at Christmas, sometimes with friends piled into station wagons and stopping in to sing and drink hot cider at others' houses.

We had our darknesses too, like anyone: the crash of my father's anger and the lost sweet notes of the farm when he made us leave it for town. Forty years later and everyone knows I will never get over that leaving. And now her clear voice silenced, and how did I never think to record her? She hated pictures of herself, but consented in her last months. She would have let me capture her talking, though by the time we knew she was dying she could not gather the breath to sing.

Christmas again soon and her favorite carol is already whispering at the edges like fog. *Lo, how a rose e'er blooming*, she sang. And there are the cardinals again, bright red against the brown grass.

Lo, how a Rose e'er blooming

trans. Theodore Baker
original: German, 15th century

Lo, how a Rose e'er blooming
From tender stem hath sprung!
Of Jesse's lineage coming,
As men of old have sung.
It came, a flow'ret bright,
Amid the cold of winter,
When half spent was the night.
Isaiah 'twas foretold it,
The Rose I have in mind;
With Mary we behold it,
The virgin mother kind.
To show God's love aright,
She bore to men a Savior,
When half spent was the night.
This Flow'r, whose fragrance tender
With sweetness fills the air,
Dispels with glorious splendor
The darkness everywhere.
True man, yet very God,
From sin and death He saves us,
And lightens every load.

Sewing and Cooking

We joked that we divided the domestic abilities: she could cook, and I could sew. Neither of us could do the other, or had any interest in it.

When she tried to sew, she got easily frustrated: threading the needle took too long, and even sewing on a button became a tangle of thread, involving multiple pricked fingers. She would come to me, or our mother, or her oldest friend, asking for a mended hem, new elastic, and yes, even a button. She disliked shopping, so she preferred to mend her clothes rather than buy new ones. One year for Christmas I made her a cardigan with lace trim on the pockets, and she wore it until it had holes, and past then.

Meanwhile, I hated cooking because it stressed me out to have to present something that other people would eat at a specific time. I worried that it wouldn't taste good, or that everything wouldn't be ready at once. Just stepping into the kitchen made me nervous, in part because when I was a young teen and our mother and my sister were away, I was supposed to cook for our father. He stood in the kitchen with me, constantly asking about whether the burner wasn't too hot, if I remembered that I had left the water in the sink running, to be careful when I chopped this, and was something burning? After that the only cooking I would do was baking easy things, like cookies or simple cakes or pies. Nothing too complicated or fussy, and everything with very precise measurements and instructions. And no one was depending on it; if it didn't come out right, it was just dessert, and we could skip that or just have ice cream.

In so many ways, we were opposites but complements. She was spontaneous, adventurous, quick to change plans if it suited her. I tend to plan, return to places I know I'll like, finish what I start. "On time" for her was no more than ten minutes late; for me, it's ten minutes early. She had difficulty making decisions; I write out pro and con lists if I need to, but make a decision quickly and decisively.

Her spontaneity, quickness to laugh, silliness, a lightness in the way she moved through the world: without that, I feel unbalanced, a boat with weight on just one side.

Ode to Her Giggle

Stone skipping across the bright water until you lose count, marveling that it could go on so long. Faceted crystals in all the colors and none, splitting and condensing light so deftly even the sun was jealous. Iced tea with fresh mint from the garden in July. Fireflies coming out of her mouth. A Stevie Wonder song so contagious you're lifting your aging joints before you even notice. Flying down a hill on the best sled anyone ever imagined. Champagne that never makes you drunk, just fizzy forever.

Beautiful

At fourteen she was taken to an experimental doctor who applied electric shock when she reached for doughnuts. She was plump, with a small waist and extra flesh above and below. Graceful, she had perfect balance atop a horse and a way of moving that made her always seem to be waltzing. I don't know who suggested this treatment, whether she agreed willingly or because she wanted to please our parents and the world.

When she was in her mid-thirties, working as a nurse with immigrant populations, she told me only that it had succeeded in one way: she hated jelly-filled doughnuts for the rest of her life.

I think there was just one session, because our parents saw that it was cruel (*barbaric*, I want to say from my viewpoint now, *insane*) and she may have gathered the courage to say she didn't want to go again.

I imagine she cried, but did what the doctor said because she was a good girl and didn't want to waste our parents' money.

Someone invented this machine, used it to try to make kids thinner. Someone tested it, probably on animals first, and then on humans. Someone could push that button, again and again, causing a sensitive young teen both pain and shame.

No one asked if she ate as a way to nurture herself while she served as a little mother to two young siblings, while our own mother could not cook or clean or watch us because of the epilepsy medications and the hours spent groggy in bed. No one asked if she needed some small pleasure to endure our father's growing anger at his own worry and helplessness, at his lack of control as he went off to work and came home to four children who created chaos by their very existence and a wife not up to the role expected of her in the 1970s.

My sister had surely heard, since she was a child, that she was chubby, fat, too big. Grandparents who had lived through the Great Depression, parents who had not yet admitted the ways society could wound and twist. I can see her trying on dresses decorated with the ruffles she loved, and our grandmother saying, "Well, that size *should* fit a little girl."

She was beautiful at any size, a peony, an envelope bringing the happy news you waited for, a clear stream on a hillside.

Her body was healthy. She played softball and volleyball and threw bales of hay down from the stack in the barn, doled them out to the horses every day.

A version of that contraption exists even now, gleaming high-tech sold on websites with the claim that you can "change your own bad habits." Shock yourself skinny! Or let a friend hold the remote control, though anyone who has heard of the Milgram experiments might be wary of bestowing that much trust.

She believed, just as so many still believe, that she could be beautiful if only she had willpower. But imagine that she, like other overweight fourteen-year-olds, used all her willpower to get out of bed in the morning, certain as she was, deep in the folds of her brain, that she was not good enough, unloved and unlovable forever. She used her willpower to face her day, in which she must simultaneously take up too much space and try to disappear so no one noticed her, smothering her ambition because a fat girl cannot aspire to much. She could not know that people would ultimately remember her for her work with disabled children and troubled teenagers at the equine therapy center she founded, while still working as a hospital chaplain to make ends meet.

Did our parents sit in that office and watch their daughter flinch and jump in pain? Or were they shuffled into a waiting room, pressed down into their chairs by the heavy hand of medical authority?

She never forgave herself for being fat, not for her whole life, and she died thinking the weight the cancer claimed made her look better—as beautiful, at last, as she had always wanted to be.

Time Travel

I go back to when she was a young child who sang made-up songs detailing her day to our mother. I am a ghost, an imprint of the future, a whisper only she can hear. *You are special,* I say. *Your imagination and joy, your voice and your spirit. Keep that always. It is beautiful. You are beautiful.*

This is before the boys bully her, try to get her to pull down her pants to show them what a girl looks like. Before she decides she will eat enough to become big, so no one will bully her again. Before she falls off the top of a slide, her first head injury.

What was lost with each successive injury? Little girl, sixteen-year-old, early 40s, and at least three more from car accidents and falling off a horse again in her 50s. What brilliance did the world miss because of a brain shaken and bruised? Girl who had made such easy *A* grades that her teachers marveled.

I cannot stop the injuries, not the one when our horse—my favorite, my mother's horse, a big chestnut who didn't mean to fall on her, who tried so hard to avoid hurting her that she did live—tripped going over a jump, not the others when cars hit her car, or when she slipped and fell on the bathroom tile because she was trying to get to the ringing phone. I cannot stop what happened to her or change what she chose, but I still go back to whisper encouragement. I float through the years and alight in an ordinary room with dust hanging in the sunbeams and I say what I can.

I go back to when our grandmother and our parents decided she was too fat, a young teenager who had an eating problem. When she eats the chocolate-covered sawdust that are her "diet bars," I whisper *You are still beautiful, you are always beautiful. You are worthy of love, you are worth every-thing good, just as you are, just as you always will be.* I do not know if she hears me. I only know years and years of men who dismiss her, treat her sometimes like a friend and sometimes like a lover. Years of her pining for men who keep her at arm's length while taking all the comfort she's willing to give. The final years with an abusive husband who yells at her and denies yelling, whose anger laps at her ankles and then her knees and sometimes her neck. The last nine months of her life, when he finally realizes what he's losing, don't make up for ten years of verbal assault, insult, blame.

What is lost when a woman undervalues herself, when men undervalue her, when even her family undervalues her?

I go back, I go back, I go back. If time isn't really linear—we just experience it that way—then I can be there, telling her everything she needs to know. *You are beautiful, your life matters, you do good just by being in the world, you deserve every joy you get, your love will buoy others in ways you may never even know.*

Sisters in Thailand

There is nothing lonelier for me than being around strangers—or people I don't know well—by myself. I need a comrade, a person who becomes a safe zone, with whom I don't have to pretend and who I trust is not judging me.

When she came with me and my first husband to Thailand for our wedding, we sat together on a bench seat in the rented van while a hired driver took us to temples and gardens. My fiancé sat behind us with his mother and aunt, and behind them often sat more aunts. She and I looked out the window at the scenery sometimes, but then often turned towards each other to talk. The conversations behind us were in Thai, which we didn't understand, making the people we knew into strangers. The signs were in Thai, and the culture was Thai. My fiancé grew tired of translating between us and his family, so we had no explanations for what we saw.

But we had each other. Facing each other like petals around the center of a tulip, we had our own world, where culture shock and my fears about marriage and not being the daughter-in-law my Thai soon-to-be relatives would want disappeared. Where she wasn't fatter than most Thai people, and hotter, and where she didn't have to ask the driver to stop so she could go to the bathroom more frequently than everyone else.

Later, in an inevitable family conflagration involving my fiancé telling his mother too much of what I'd said to him about my physical and emotional discomfort, she told him she disliked how my sister and I sat turned away from the windows of the van, as if we were rejecting Thailand. How our bubble of sisterhood made her feel outcast.

Coma

I didn't panic when people went into the hospital 30 minutes away; Mom did sometimes after a seizure, returning the same day or the next with new stitches in her head. I had been in it after I'd fallen from a tree and opened my eyes to a neighbor's serious-faced Great Danes hovering over me as I lay on the couch, vaguely wondering if they'd carried me there. But the morning I woke up without my sister in the other twin bed across the room, I remembered everyone's faces the night before, knotted as the faces you sometimes saw in wood grain, and I worried.

She had not fallen off Crest, our big chestnut Morgan gelding, while practicing taking him over jumps in the lower pasture; he had caught his hoof on a jump and fallen onto her. At least 1,000 pounds of horse landed on her, and yet she lived. Our mother and I believed that Crest had done everything he could not to crush her, because we both knew how well he could care for a rider. When our mother had a seizure either while riding or near him, he stood over her, protecting her from any harm, until she came to and told him it was okay. When I put on his bridle, he lowered his head so I could reach and opened his mouth for the bit. He didn't even fill his belly with air when I tried to tighten the girth, pitting my small self against buckles that fastened over my head. He loved us, and somehow he shifted his weight as fast as possible to get off her. Also, she was wearing a hardhat, a requirement on our farm that our friends sometimes complained about; the hardhat was broken when they took it off her.

I remember a week with no parents, just babysitters and neighbor moms trading off. I heard the word "coma" and knew generally what it meant, though not that she might never wake up. I remember that I wasn't allowed to visit her in the hospital, so I imagined a small room with her in a hospital bed, my parents and a nurse leaning over her, the windows dark. It was always dark when she was there, in my imagination.

She spent a lot of time in bed after she came home, and I realized enough to let her call my cocker spaniel onto her bed each night instead of bickering in our usual way. Always playful, often unpredictable, she became even more unpredictable, begging me to kiss her big toe before we went to sleep. She said it with a joke in her voice, but she kept asking, and she would not go to sleep until I did it. And if anyone even mentioned an itchy nose, or touched their own nose, she rubbed and rubbed at hers, feeling an itch she could never reach, some misrouted nerve or faulty connection from the concussion that would last her entire life. Luckily it got milder, possible for her to resist over the years, unless one of our brothers said, "Hey sis!" and rubbed their own noses. She'd say, "Oh, no!" and turn away, calling them jerks (or worse) but unable to block out that cue.

What I didn't know then, eight years old to her sixteen, was how much she lost. School had been so easy for her. She had no weak subjects. Teachers loved her, how she turned in her homework on time, how her mind leapt from idea to idea like a dragonfly landing on stems of grass. Math, Latin, English, art—she never struggled. She was heading towards a college scholarship for her grades and test scores. She was shy, insecure, plump, but her mind was a fine instrument, effortless to play.

Until after the accident.

A severe concussion can cause a number of symptoms. The ones I know she had included depression, difficulty concentrating, difficulty finding things, difficulty reading, being easily distracted, feeling overwhelmed, getting lost easily, irritability, sensitivity to loud noises and complex visual experiences, short-term memory issues, difficulty with decisions, difficulty planning, changes in mood and personality. Some of these eased over the weeks and months, so that it became easier to read, focus, and remember things. She was able to graduate high school on time with decent grades and get into an excellent state university.

But some of the things we all teased her about—her abysmal sense of direction, startling ability to get lost while driving, and inevitable lateness—were almost certainly not inherent parts of her, but results of her head injury. When I became a professor and students arrived to class five, ten, or fifteen minutes late, I was irritated at having to repeat myself and at what I considered disrespect. I didn't learn that this was a classic symptom of traumatic brain injury until I'd been teaching for well over ten years. Her accident occurred in the 70s. Few knew then just how profoundly and permanently a brain injury could affect a person. So she grew up wearing the symptoms of this injury like the clanking tin cans tied to the back of a newlywed couple's car, with everyone around her assuming she could just cut the strings and free herself. Even the people who loved her, family and friends, served their fond jokes with a side of blame.

Hanami (Viewing the Cherry Blossoms)

When she lived in Washington, D.C., with our grandmother, a sweet man who had asked to "court her" took her down to the cherry trees one evening in early April with a Walkman and two headsets. They danced under those pink and white petals. I thought she would marry him after that, but his energy flagged and though they lived together for a time, they fought and picked at each other. She wanted more of those romantic outings, more exploration and adventure; he wanted to play online games with friends he had never met in person.

*

Grandmommy (she thought "Grandma" was too "rural") was dying of lung cancer, having picked up cigarettes in the 1920s when she was at college and never put them down. Her husband died when our mother was fourteen, and she never remarried, so when we knew her she lived in an apartment on an upper floor with a view of Rock Creek Park. I remember how strange it felt to get to that apartment, to take an elevator up and walk blank halls only to open a door and be inside a *house*. She had a kitchen, living room, dining room, two bedrooms, two bathrooms. Since we grew up in a green house in the countryside of Illinois, it seemed like a magic trick that there were actual living spaces tucked into tall buildings, almost like I'd opened a door in a tree and discovered a house in every branch.

*

Once, towards the end of her life, she heard my sister singing in the hallway and thought the angels had finally come for her.

*

Once, when our mother was visiting, she threw a glass of cold water on my sister in the shower—one of our mother's impish tricks—and Grandmommy, still mobile, threw a glass of water on our mother in the hallway. Our mother always told the story by saying, "And I was *fully clothed*!"

*

My sister was unimaginably young then, still in her 20s. How did she get chosen or volunteer to oversee our grandmother's dying? How does a girl that age decide she can serve as emotional support for a dying elder, watch her decline, feed her pills, decide when our mother should come out because *it* was going to happen soon?

*

In her 40s, my sister finally married a different man, one who wooed her with hikes in the mountains and dog walks and weekly dancing. When she died in her late 50s, he had curbed his anger for precisely nine months, from her cancer diagnosis to her death.

*

I went with her to the cherry trees during the blossoming season, though I don't remember whether it was before or after she went with her beau. We walked among monuments, made it to the Lincoln Memorial—our favorite, since our home state was Illinois—and felt somehow like the whole fragrant scene was ours alone.

*

I inherited much of the silver and fancy china from Grandmommy; our father's mother had liked pink glassware and delicate white plates with pink roses, and so her things went to my sister. That grandmother died in a nursing home, her husband having watched her walk down the lonely road of Alzheimer's.

*

My sister could sit beside a patient's bed and that person would feel her calm and compassion rolling over them like powerful perfume. Where did she learn to do that? When I'm confronted by suffering I feel jagged and spiky, self-conscious and useless.

*

Away from the sickbed she might return to her prickly self, assuming ill intent in relatives' words that seemed innocuous to me. She might duck responsibility, fail to plan ahead, overuse the word *stress* when she really meant *anger* or *exhaustion* or *fear* or *self-loathing*. Away from the sickbed, she was challenging, someone I worried about and protected myself from in equal measure.

*

The first cherry trees sent over from Japan were infected with insects and had to be destroyed. Are they blooming in my grandmother's heaven? In my sister's?

Shaman

She planted like a profligate, buying flowers and vegetables like someone gathering beads at Mardi Gras. She would find a place for them, she just knew. The muscle and bone work of caring for plants a pleasure until it became pain, her old bad knee aching, the sun she loved too hot, the bending and straightening again and again and never knowing what to do with the pulled weeds. Her back porch was a riot of half-alive plants, potatoes going wild as if they could return to South America long before the Spanish came like I knew she sometimes wished to: a time and place without computers or paper money, people more connected to what they could touch.

Though I think she was always a shaman. In Africa they found crystals associated with humans 105,000 years ago. Some must have felt the energy of them as she did, holding her hand over a rock and smiling. Once we were talking about a young man with mental illness and I said the way he talked about God must be a symptom, as if God was right there like another human in the room. She said He was, she could always feel Him.

Some things I want to believe in, and some I don't. It's spring again, and I am about to go out to my back garden and speak to all my plants by name.

A brother's dream

Just so you know I dream of her about once a month. It is such a vivid dream and I'm always surprised to see her and I wonder how she is back but I am so happy to see her! It is strange and confusing in my dream but exciting to see her. One of my first dreams was her walking out of the horse pasture in a fog but when she got closer it was not her but someone who looked just like her and I was left longing to see her again.

—Text from our youngest brother

Gone

My sister is dead. This is a fact that I want everyone to know: strangers, acquaintances, friends I haven't talked to in a year or more. I feel like part of me has been amputated but no one can see it; the illusion is too good. I am not what I once was. She and I spoke on the phone daily, often more than once. She called when she was driving to work as a hospital chaplain, or back home to work with troubled kids at her equine therapy center, or as she drove to visit a parishioner who was ill or grieving, either a member of the church she attended or the one she co-pastored. The word *busy* is too short to describe the multisyllables of her everyday life.

Meanwhile for the past eight years I have sat at home writing poems, doing a little editing, teaching small online classes (independent, ungraded), and playing with our pets. After teaching in universities for over 20 years, I finally left that game, defeated and unable to escape the smell of my failure to rise to tenure-track, let alone tenure. I moved to a different state to get married and left the constant reminders of my lesser-than status behind.

My sister helped give my suddenly center-less life meaning and purpose. She gave so much of herself to others, and I supported her. I shored her up as she struggled with a difficult marriage, worries about money, and the tides and breakers of other people's suffering. I tread the line between listening sympathetically to her escapist fantasies—maybe she'd take a part-time job in Florida, move there with her four dogs, surely there was someplace she could rent; or she'd peruse real estate listings near me in Memphis, scheming ways to buy a house—and discouraging them with too much realism. If I just listened and said, "Interesting," she'd ask me why I wasn't enthusiastic enough. If I told her what I thought she really needed to do in order to start a new life, she quickly got off the phone. Being her confidante and advisor wasn't always easy.

But she also asked how I was, cared about the tiny challenges and triumphs of my days. I'd gotten a poem accepted—celebration! The herbs I'd planted in pots outdoors died—sympathy and good gardening advice. And anything that involved interpersonal relationships, such as how to give my new husband and his teenage daughter space while keeping my own sense of self-worth—empathy and the wisdom of years spent helping people in just these kinds of ways, compounded by how well she knew me, her little sister.

Anger

Her husband was like those rolled green wire fences from the home improvement store, the ones not tall enough to keep a big dog out of the flower garden but enough of a barrier to discourage trampling. Those rolls are held together with an unknown number of fasteners, which must be clipped with wire cutters to release the roll. But you don't know how many fasteners there are, and how tightly wound the fence is. You lean over it with the clippers, knowing it'll eventually spring open, not knowing when. Once it does start to expand/ unroll, sometimes you can stop it and sometimes you can't, and there's always the fear that it'll open so fast the end will fling out and strike you in the eye, or maybe just under it, giving you the chance to say to people for days how lucky you were that you could still see.

Torn

When our father had his breakdown, my sister called me daily, sometimes several times a day. I had just gotten my first cell phone so she could reach me anywhere. Having grown up in the time before answering machines, I still felt I should answer the phone whenever it rang.

"Hey Weirdy," I said. My stomach felt like it wasn't in the right spot in my body, like when the rollercoaster sent you plunging. "What's up?"

"He doesn't sound good. He's afraid of everything," she said. It was always bad news then. "I'm trying to find out if M has gotten a second opinion. I can't believe she put him in a mental facility."

I don't know what I said. Every conversation was like this, and I was helpless—living across the country, unable or unwilling to talk to Dad's partner, teaching part-time, but enough that I couldn't leave my job to go back to Illinois to do anything anyway. I probably said something about how hard it was, agreed that M was, if not evil, then at least far from a good person, and told her I loved her.

After she called while my first husband and I were trying out new mattresses and I answered, getting up from the one we were lying on to see if we liked it, he told me I needed to set some boundaries: no answering the phone when we were out together, and no answering the phone during meals.

It was the beginning of the boundaries I had to set with her. She wanted all the time I was willing to give, and the cell phone made that so much more complicated. I was relieved that my husband had pushed me to make that rule for myself—for us—and I was also guilty. She was trying to save our dad. She needed me, because she was always doing something to help others, her jobs ranging from nurse at a Spanish-speaking center in Washington, D.C., to public health to volunteering in Guatemala. I felt it was my obligation to support her as she helped others.

But I couldn't live that way, torn between her and my husband, always feeling like her time was more important than mine, guilty for not doing enough, and resenting it all at the same time.

All Things Bright and Beautiful

I'm in England, visiting my husband-to-be Andy's family for the first time, the second time, the third time. Trips to different parts of Yorkshire every day, the moors with their dry-stone walls vaguely familiar from the original series of *All Creatures Great and Small*, a show my mother, sister, and I watched in the TV room of our central Illinois farmhouse, often while we polished bridles and other tack for the horses. Andy's mother, one of the first women veterinarians in England, knew James Herriot, and when we were first getting to know each other, he blithely used this fact to impress me. I'm in love with Andy and England, strong tea drunk over conversation or scones with clotted cream, 65-degree summer days, heather blooming purple on the hillsides.

Andy has worked my cell phone so I can't receive calls on my regular number, but I have data so I can post photos to social media, get emails, and receive texts on an internet-based number. When we're at his parents' house, I can make an audio or video call using their wireless internet.

I get a text from my sister. *Can you call? Hope you're having a great time.*

My stomach tightens. I have enjoyed being away from my regular life, immersed in vacation. It is a time when every call with my sister involves a crisis: there's conflict with the girl helping out with the horses, or her husband has yelled at her in front of riding clients again, or one of the dogs is sick and she doesn't know if she can afford to take it to the vet. When I think of her, I'm sick with worry and rage and helplessness. I want her to stop the equine therapy program, sell all the horses except the two she inherited from our mother, kick her husband out of the house. I want peace for her, happiness, leisure time, love.

I call her. "What's up? Is everything okay?"

"Yes," she says. "I just wanted to hear your voice."

"You're weird," I say, our standard tease. "I slipped down a mud bank today. Andy almost pulled a muscle laughing."

"What are you doing now?"

"It's evening here. Just sitting in the bedroom upstairs, looking out at the moors."

"Sounds like heaven."

"So how is everything at your place?"

She tells me. It's actually not as bad talking with her about the problems as ruminating on them. I repeat myself a lot: *I am so sorry that happened. Of course anyone would be upset if they got yelled at like that. It's not okay for you to be treated that way. I wish I knew what to suggest.*

It's difficult to recreate a typical scene where her husband behaved badly, in part because it was so instinctive for me to shut down, disappear, as I had in childhood when our father raged. But I'd stayed with them for nearly a year when I was separating from my first husband; I knew how she lived. Her husband's overly loud, angry, condescending tone was like a physical blow. His body moved in jerky, angry fits. His fists balled and his chin jutted forward. The words? They hardly mattered. He could have said, "It's a nice day today" and it would still have been a lash, a punishment. It would still have implied that everything bad in his life was her fault. Once, when she got in a car accident—admittedly one of several—he came to pick her up, furious. He didn't ask if she was okay, or how she was feeling. She asked if he was angry at her for having an accident, and he said, "Yes. Why shouldn't I be?"

When we hang up, I sit on the bed for a few minutes, breathing, trying to calm myself down. It's not only that I'm feeling awful for my sister, but for any innocent who comes in contact with her husband when he's radiating anger like that: the kid with Down Syndrome who witnessed him yelling at her, the horses, the dogs. He doesn't hit the animals—he's actually a little afraid of the horses—but he makes them wait until he's good and ready, and hurls down their food bowls. Rescued bichon needs to go outside to pee? She has to wait. No water in any of the dog water bowls? He'll fill them when he has to get up again for something else.

Any mistreatment of animals, even minimal neglect, hurts me. It's been that way my whole adult life. But I suspect I also imagine the animals absorbing his anger the way my sister does, becoming wounded as she is, their natural confidence and exuberance shrinking, as hers is.

Downstairs I try to explain to Andy and his parents. How I cannot get her to take the steps necessary to divorce him. How her indecision makes me frustrated with her, when really it's her I want to protect. How even if I knew what to do to help, her situation is complicated and difficult financially. She can't leave—they're her horses, her four rescued dogs. And she's afraid to tell him to leave. She couldn't afford the farm without his financial and physical help, and I'm broke, chronically ill, and unemployed, relying on Andy's job to get us through as we try to pay off debts accumulated during our first marriages.

The beds in Andy's parents' guest room are twins, so when we go up to sleep, I cannot stay burrowed into him all night. Eventually I move back to my own narrow bed, hoping I can forget my sister's situation for at least some of the day tomorrow, while I walk the moors she and I first glimpsed together on a small, fuzzy TV screen forty years ago. I cannot know that by the time the new series comes out she will have been dead for over a year, cancer taking her as swiftly as it took our mother, that as I watch it I will wish I had stolen her from her difficult life and brought her here, that some small shameful part of me will be relieved for us both that her suffering is over and my inability to help her finally absolute.

Trying to Rescue Dad

When our father had his breakdown, my sister essentially kidnapped him and brought him out East. She was living in Washington, D.C., and I was living in upstate New York with my first husband.

Our father was a ball of worry, a string someone had unraveled and then tried clumsily to twine, knots and loops everywhere. He thought the attendants at the gas station were going to come out, disable the car, and kill him and anyone he was riding with; he worried that the men working on the house next door were secret agents for Russia, spying on him, presenting an unspecified danger. He had said to our mother that his partner, the second woman he had dated since our parents split, would find out he didn't have as much money as she thought and when she did, she would cut his balls off.

My sister persuaded him to take a trip with her. I don't know how she persuaded his partner, a woman who I've thought at different times was a sociopath, a narcissist, stupid, bewildered, selfish, cruel, controlling, greedy, and petty. My sister wanted to save Dad from her, believing that part of his breakdown could be attributed to his realization of who he had connected himself with, moved into a brand-new expensive house with, paid for with his retirement money, IRAs squirreled away while he and our mother raised four kids and bought generic toilet paper.

She showed up at our log cabin in Oswego with Dad. He was pleased to be there, sweet to me and the dogs, kind to my husband. But his face was permanently molded into an expression of fear, eyebrows pushed together, mouth small.

They arrived on a Friday, after she was off work, and had to return to D.C. on Sunday. We put it off as long as we could, but on Saturday evening, she and I sat in the finished basement with Dad and tried to find out what he wanted and if there was anything real for him to fear from his partner. If he said to us, "I don't want to be with her," or "Please don't make me go back to her," we would know. Then maybe we could help him.

She sat beside him, holding his hand. I was afraid. Madness scared me. Rationality helped me trust other people and the world. Irrationality meant anything could happen—a hidden knife suddenly brought out, a painful secret revealed, words spoken that could reverberate like a sacred fortune even if they were never true.

"Can you tell me how you're doing, Dad?" she asked.

"Okay," he said. "Glad to be here with you two."

"How do you feel about the idea of going home?" I asked. The basement was cold, even with the heat coming through vents overhead.

"I don't know," he said.

"You've said some things about the new house. It seems to worry you," I said.

He said he didn't know, didn't remember. We both tried to get him to say what he wanted, what he was really afraid of. He didn't know.

"Do you want to sell the house, live somewhere else?" I asked, finally. "Are you sure you want to live with M?"

"It's a nice house," he said.

She and I looked at each other. He never said that he didn't want to go home, that he was afraid of her. Hours of stressful conversations with our brothers had made the possibility of declaring him mentally incompetent to manage his own affairs seem extremely difficult, especially since the court would see it as us not wanting to share any of his money with his current partner. Our mother, still married to him for health insurance, did not want to get dragged into a messy court case.

I shook my head, and turned the conversation to something easy for him, something about my dogs, silly spaniels that loved to sit by him on the couch.

She had tried to save him, and she did not give up easily. There were still hours of stressful phone calls ahead, plans and possibilities, frustration and sadness. But I knew the campaign was over. And I always felt that I had let *her* down that day, not him. And once more, as seemed to happen over and over in our lives, she had taken action when I hadn't. She had stepped in, tried to help, her empathy pushing her to act while mine mostly kept me frozen.

You Should Know Her

The thing is, you should know my sister. You should want to know her. How many of Whitman's contradictions she embodied. She studied anthropology and sociology in college, went to seminary, dropped out, went to nursing school, worked as a nurse for troubled teens, pregnant teens, Spanish speakers, immigrants, the rural poor. Had two car accidents that shook her brain inside her skull, bruising it like an overripe peach, went on disability, went back to seminary. She worked as a hospital chaplain and started an equine therapy center on her farm, running on a shoestring budget and relying on her scheduling skills, which were weak. Finally got a part-time pastor job at a small rural church, was denied ordination, worked hard, was finally ordained. Made it to her installation service at the small church directly from the hospital. Died a month later.

Facts, I know. So boring. The thing is, the inside of her lit up—like when you put a flashlight inside a balloon—when she helped people who needed it. When she sat with a family whose child had died. When she spoke with new mothers, listened to the dying. When she calmly asked a pre-teen why she'd behaved as she had, storming off in the middle of the horse-riding lesson—and then listened so well the kid was back with the group in a few minutes. She shone when people were in need, gliding through conversations tangled up with loss and anger and blame as if it took no effort at all to smooth those gnarled yarns. I never knew how she did it, self-conscious as I was, always certain I'd say the wrong thing, be unwelcome as hot sun to those sunburned red and raw. She managed to be both light and shade, whatever was needed, simply by stepping into the room.

And yet—religious but open-minded, spiritual in ways that fit with both shamans and priests. Accustomed to helping people grieving or stuck, but the silliest player of board games ever, her giggle infectious. The most active of listeners, but stubborn as an old nail.

Cherry Tomatoes

Do you remember when she and I found the cherry tomato plant loaded with red orbs in front of the fire station where our brother worked and we picked and ate, picked and ate?

What fun thing are you going to do today?

She asked me on the phone, nearly every day, *What fun thing are you going to do today?* She made me answer. *Laundry,* I'd say, sometimes, just to tease her.

Nope. That's not fun.

Not even if I'm out of clean underwear?

Gross. Don't even tell me.

*Let's just say…*I'd start.

No! She'd fake-shriek. *No!*

Andy will be happy when he gets home.

And we'd laugh, and she wouldn't know that was my fun thing, making her laugh.

But seriously, she'd say. *Tell me. And laundry doesn't count.*

Brave

Did I say she was brave? So easy for her to stand up for anyone but herself. Or not easy—she didn't talk about the stones pressed into her flesh, invisible, the hardness and the weight and the bruises. Leaving the dinner table, our father's anger trailing after her like smoke. Sitting with our grandmother as she died, volunteering in Guatemala before she spoke Spanish, listening to teenagers whose rage and shame cut new wounds in the world. She called to tell me my dog died, and lifetimes later when our mother and then our father died. Bearing the news to someone you love is like running into a burning building to save them: both of you will come out hurt, throats sore and raspy. More than all that she was brave enough to seek joy. Too many times I let my watch rule me, stayed too straight to the path. If she had not driven into the forest, our supply of gasoline dwindling, no phones for miles, eight hours of driving behind us and three more before home, would I remember that trip? The sun slanting through the trees, her faith that we would find our way out.

College

Do I need to tell you what happened to her in college, a girl as innocent as a violet and as easy to overlook? She was round in the 70s and shy. She'd grown up in a place where she knew everyone in her grade, every year since fourth grade. When she went off to a state school in the freshly-minted year of Reagan's presidency, she had never been drunk. She didn't know what boys could do. What they would do.

I didn't know then what had happened, but I remember my mother's face when she was on the phone. She was so angry she was like a comet heading for Earth, bent on extinction. Angrier, because the cosmic winds diverted her. She could not exact revenge, but she could bring my sister home, to go to the university in our town.

When I taught college, I saw the same kind of damage in the eyes of young women as my sister came home with. Sometimes they wrote about it in poems or stories. Sometimes they quietly dropped out, and I never knew what happened to them.

My sister never said anything to me about it, not once in forty years.

Tough

When I was in college and she was home in between one of her many jobs, she blew out her knee playing softball. I was on the same team—summer recreational—and I saw it happen. She was running to home base, and her knee just buckled. It didn't look like anything terrible, but it swelled up and she was nearly crying in pain. Mom and I took her home, but when it didn't improve, Mom took her to the doctor. It was a mess inside, torn ligament, jumbled cartilage. She had surgery, and six weeks of recovery and physical therapy. The physical therapy hurt so much it made her cry, but she did it, even at home on the couch, and she recovered faster than they thought she would. In between, she and I played Yahtzee, hours spent rolling dice. I always kept score.

Recurring dream

We have to go to a formal event. This time it is an award ceremony for our brother. We came to this city unprepared, wearing only our usual clothes: me in jeans and a t-shirt, her in turquoise cropped pants and a lacy shirt. An acquaintance brings us to her apartment and opens her closet, lets us choose something. Why some of our old dresses are there, we don't know. Time is short: the event begins in less than an hour. We must select something quickly, but we don't know what will still fit of those old, outdated things. *I'd forgotten this skirt,* I say. *I thought I'd lost this shawl,* she says. I have gained weight; it looks like I might have to wear pink, one of her old dresses. I never wear pink, but we must get there, and look presentable. She has lost weight, but my old things are too dark, army-green and somber, and too long-waisted. She looks like a little kid in them, the tunic tops erasing her figure. We look at each other, panicked. There is not enough time. There is never enough time.

III

She Sings Like Light

The neighbor's got some extra loud power tool going a few houses over and it sounds like a big bass drum. Music's everywhere: my dog snoring beside me, the chime of a text from my sister, the sunlight oozing like blues through the window. Don't discount modern technology: she's at work helping the sick and their families cope—dying mothers, car accidents, living wills—her prayers and presence calming. While she struggles to breathe, something vicious in her lungs that the doctors are treating too slowly and the hospital administrators won't give her time off for. I am so angry the metal hammer of my heart is sparking as it comes down. I wish I could say something is being created in there, swords for the revolution or horseshoes or the tiny parts of music boxes like the ones my grandfather collected. Instead it's just that big bass drum doing nothing but shouting its existence while someone I love suffers, while suffering wheezes words no one wants to hear and the rest of us make the choice we must make every day: despair or life, to keep turning that little handle so the unknowable melody tinkles out note after note after note.

After her diagnosis, I don't know what to do with my hands. My feet ache. The light is gray now but I suspect it would be gray even if it were gold. I am lonely already, and she is still alive, if only for a short time (any known time is too short). I think I have forgotten how to talk to people. People are divided into two categories: those who know and those who don't. I am already tired of telling those who know more details about tumors and treatment and her state of mind. She is radiant with beauty and acceptance, and also blank with shock. She worries about her 120-pound shaggy white dog, her heart-child. I think I have forgotten how to feel in my own heart, it seems physical only, pumping as though it belongs to a stranger. It is spring and migrating birds come through the back yard. I love the Rose-breasted Grosbeak for the splash of pink-red on its chest. If I were wounded with a spear I would want to look like that.

Against advice, she delays chemo. There is so little time. But she wants to see if the other treatment might be better, the one that requires DNA sequencing. Give me a hammer and a chisel and I will get to work on the tumors. I will sculpt her down to her essence of little girl barrettes and servant of God (capitalization hers). No one will see the suffering on her face in this or any life. In the first session with the nurse—the same day her prognosis was delivered—she worried about getting a port for the chemo because she gets keloid scar tissue. She didn't want the ugly scar on her chest. And though it hurt me to think it I thought *Why worry when you have so little time?* And then I thought, *It will show where you have been struck by lightning, chosen or cursed by gods I find easier than the one you love.* And I thought, *Please,* and I didn't know if I was begging her or something else, but I kept my mouth shut, thin and straight as a line.

Tequila Never Helps but It Doesn't Hurt

I am not courageous. If I were dying, I'd save up the pills so when I hurt too much I could speed things along. In daydreams that go wrong—kidnap, torture, suffering—I find a way to kill myself. The easy way out, a voice says inside. But if I'm flying towards that big window anyway, I'm going forward with all my speed—and if it's glass and closed then I won't care if there's anyone to smooth my feathers, check my eyes for life on this side. If there's another side I hope it's mostly soaring. I want to ask my sister what she thinks it is, but do you ask that kind of thing of the dying? She believes something, though I can't remember ever talking about it. Why can't I remember? Does she believe she'll see our parents, grandparents, lost dogs, past horses? My old friend hopes there's no reincarnation, doesn't want to wake up in a crib and think, "Dammit!" Which makes me laugh. Which makes me take another sip of my margarita, feel the cold slide down my throat. The trees are in full leaf. My sister has few seasons left. And I must stay alive for all of them.

Beginning with a Line from James Wright

When I went out to kill myself—the brittle brown leaves in late summer, the dry wind, the dying all around but mostly the ugliness in me, my blunt and clumsy pain—I grew tired and instead of completing the journey, I lay down on the road. There were many of us there, lying with our heads on our arms, exhausted. My sister said it was difficult—strange—to host a church service for someone who had committed suicide, an acquaintance, when she was trying so hard to live. What she meant was that she was angry! And why not? No one's sorrow is greater than any other, most of us who've been on that road just as worthy as any other flawed/flayed human. Now I don't want to die, even metaphorically, but I feel so sad it sometimes drowns me. I have learned to suspend breathing, to look around under the waves because I have to get used to living here. I have to get used to living without my calico cat, crushed in front of my eyes, and the millions of birds disappeared since my childhood in the 1970s. She has not yet lost her hair from the chemo. I am ashamed but sometimes she must have enough faith for us all, her anger an anchor, her hair drifting like a mermaid's.

Astronomy

Today I'm sad but then I see an article about the universe and I slip into star-time and everything isn't so scary. I wonder if astronomers are happier than the rest of us because of this. If time and distances are so vast that what is here and now can be perceived as miniscule, fleeting as the belief that you remember birth, every sorrow nearly disappearing in the shadows of other stars and the stranger phenomena: nebulae, quasars, supernovas... Astronomers deal in math and squinting through tubes and the inside of their heads must be pinpricks of light spread out in patterns the rest of us can't even imagine, moving like leaves in wind or ripples on a puddle but in more dimensions. Oh to have those bright spacescapes within, nothing like the patch of wildflowers and clover in front of my sister's house where she sits—sun on her thinned face, the cancer not yet keeping her in bed, her pain not yet so great that it hurts me to see it—that place where she will always be, even after someone mows it, and that particular sun goes dark.

Buying a Piece of Bluestone for My Sister

In England, the years speak—even to me, all fresh and pink in my Americanness. *Slow down*, they say. *It takes hundreds to move the stones.* England measures time in millennia, so a few minutes make no difference. *Go to the pub, talk, say you're leaving, don't get up, talk some more.* In America we are always leaving the past like it's going to stand up and bite us again. I admit this country is intoxicating: moor and cathedral, dates etched in stone. Voices out of books, roses so damned easy to grow. This is the land that nurtured my love, the place he grew up. I cling to him, out of breath on a walk into hills. Back home, in the flat center of America, my sister is dying. *Slow down*, I say. But the place where she lives—lovely, too, though harsher—does not listen.

I like a dog with dark brown eyes. I like trees that shake in the wind like a dog just out of a bath. Few sweets will go untasted if I'm around, though like my mom I always thought cotton candy a waste—merely spun sugar. Give me hearty flavors: chocolate, salted caramel, mint, blackberry. I love the sun when it's 65 and I'm walking around a lake in England, Highland cows witnessing. I like birdwatching but I don't have a life list; the ones I see every day are friends whose names I like to say again and again. I like making my sister laugh, especially now that she's got cancer and chemo's kicking the shit out of her. I guess what I'm saying is there are things I like about life, so why the fear when I drive over bridges, the knowledge that inside me is someone who has thought about turning that wheel, about how easy it is to almost fly when you're actually falling fast?

Mallie

Our beloved calico cat, Mallie, died under the wheels of our own car. We had spent hours looking for her in the house and in the garage, even taking a flashlight to look under the cars. When my husband decided he had to go to work, I stood in the driveway to watch for Mallie, in case she ran out (she was an inside-only cat). I saw her drop out from some hidden place in the underbody of his car and run right under the wheel as he was slowly backing out. There was nothing either of us could do. Though we rushed to the vet, she died on the way.

The next day, my sister drove the six and a half hours down from Illinois. She was so sick she had to stop to throw up.

We were devastated, numb. We could not do anything for her; she came merely to be with us in our trauma and grief. Three and a half months before she died, she was taking care of others. She just sat with us as we watched mindless TV, chewed our food.

When I cried—that sweet little calico body had laid against my heart as I first took in my sister's terminal diagnosis, had tunneled under the covers to capture my husband's warmth at night—my sister told me it was okay, it was normal, it was good to let it out. Mallie, still small and kitten-like at two, had been what she called a bright spirit.

She stayed a couple of days and then had to drive back to Illinois for more doctor's appointments, more chemo.

She came to take care of us. She always did.

My Memory Shack

In this room of time—the one I am trapped in right now, though it will eventually have discrete walls and one dreadful exit—my sister is dying from cancer. As my mother did. What good are all these rooms if the doors only open onto more loss? Every memory tacked on to the next by an inexpert carpenter, the floors ramshackle enough I might fall through to the room below so suddenly I'm in my twin bed with the blue calico bedspread that matches my sister's and we're arguing lightly about who gets the cocker spaniel on her bed for the beginning of the night and it's the cusp of summer so the window lets in the breath of trees and the possibility of the stars falling into the grass to become fireflies flashing, flashing for all they're worth—telegraphing their brief and beautiful lives.

Doctors

My sister, not usually timid, follows the rules when talking to her oncologist: you may ask a question, but do not press for explanations. *Is surgery or radiation possible for the masses in my abdomen?*

No, ma'am, he said, shaking his head.

I was not there, or I would like to think I would have pressed, pushed, shoved until we knew. Couldn't they make her feel a little better before she dies? After all, I was the one who had asked during that first diagnosis, when we heard the masses in her lungs had proliferated, alighted in more and more spots: what's the prognosis? How much more time does she have? As if to say it twice was to get ahead, somehow, of the answer. As if having the massive weight of her mortality dropped all at once could rule out fear. As if all the questions don't come down to *why*, every time.

It's worse not to know. She lives in a small town. There are worse oncologists, like the one who, faced with more symptoms than just her severe anemia, said *Not my problem.* Her diagnosis delayed by months. My head feels like a can of pennies when I think about it, but she will not let anger rule her. She is too tired. She has lost so much weight that she must buy all new clothes.

When she told me this, she said the doctor spoke with regret, his brows pushed together. I held my phone to my ear, imagined his forehead furrowed, like a plowed field in central Illinois where she lives and the farmers grow corn one year, soybeans the next. I wanted to punch him then, not for the news but for the imprecision of it. When our mother went from pancreatic cancer, she hit her six-month mark almost exactly. Shouldn't there be rules for doctors too? To tell the most accurate and complete truth they can?

Nourishment

The old cat lies on the old dog's bed—we both miss her, chestnut fur and gray muzzle. Hard to believe the dog I inherited from our mother died this year, the year of my sister's cancer. My sister, like my mother did, shrinks sometimes like a rose unblooming and sometimes like a blade sharpened so much it begins to disappear.

Of the three of us women in the family only my sister was a feeder, a cook. Now she cannot eat and when she does she cannot hold the food inside her. And though my throat is stopped daily as the expectation of grief runs through me like electric shock waves, somehow I grow round and thick. I stuff my mouth to knock down the rising panic. I feed myself all the pleasure she can no longer have, as if I can fortify myself against the coming famine, as if that kind of nourishment is what I will need.

PO

My sister's oldest friend sends me a quilted card—real fabric—and I choke when I open the envelope, knowing we're both just making thousands of tiny stitches to try to hold ourselves together. It's still a miracle that we can put something in a box in our own town and let others drive it across fields of cotton that give way eventually to corn, though one of the little items of news I keep hearing is that the Post Office is going away. And then my sister gets sicker, the cancer moving like a vine through her abdomen, strangling the delicate system of stomach and intestine, and time loops and twists as well so on the next occasion I am opening cards sent through the mail she is gone, vacuumed into some other existence.

Prey

Wasps live inside her bones, her lungs, her abdomen. Her oncologist gives partial answers, listens to half of what she says. He thinks of himself as an exterminator, though he's told her this structure is too infested, it will collapse in perhaps a year. Maybe because she's a lost cause, he's not willing to come too close, risk getting swarmed.

We want to know what can be done to reduce the pain. It's not like getting stung to death, she tells me. It's pressure and nausea, fatigue like she's carrying something far too heavy. My job is to make her laugh, listen when she can't stand the way others behave around her: cloying, like the smell of chemicals someone is attempting to cover up.

Have you ever looked inside a paper wasp nest? The rows of open cells like windows in a high rise. She's a country girl. In nature, there are rules. Every nest built to certain shapes, according to species. Every predator something's prey. We just haven't yet found what hunts the masses multiplying inside her.

While Standing on Your Head

Before the babysitter came, my mother often said, "If she tells you to stand on your head and sing the Star-Spangled Banner backwards, you do it!" I hoped she wouldn't, because I couldn't sing that song even forwards, though I thought I could stand on my head for a little while.

For nine months, between my sister's diagnosis and her death, I shredded my worry like a tissue and reshaped it into anything else when I spoke to her. I made her laugh and it made me proud. I knew she was caring for me as well, doing the hard work of dying while still singing so others could hear.

Spending a Life

Even when we don't talk about it, we talk about it. There's how she's feeling (tired, nauseated) and how she's feeling after chemo (utterly exhausted, unable to eat or drink, vomiting blood, requiring IV fluids). There are doctor appointments where male oncologists ignore her questions, compete with each other for the right treatment. There are meds and alternative meds, a chatty acupuncturist whose ministrations help more than the anti-nausea pills.

She is less interested in her disease than in what she can manage to do: how many troubled teens can she work with at her equine therapy center in a week, how many parishioners of the church she co-pastors she can visit in the hospital, how many friends and family seen or talked to on the phone. I often think she tries to do too much, bankrupting her energy supply. But then, I always did think she did too much, packing activities into the minutes between other activities, arriving late because she'd been coordinating a service or offering solace. Her best paying job was working as a chaplain in a hospital, and she still sometimes works a couple of hours here or there, leading group meditation classes or just sitting with patients.

She also doesn't dwell on the outcome of her disease. She has stage IV lung cancer. She has expressed no fear of death, which does not surprise me given her strong faith. But she has *so much to do*, she wants as much time as possible in which to do it. And unlike my own to-do list (#1: PET ALL THE DOGS), in addition to helping people, she wants to spend time with family and friends. My husband and I are taking her to the beach—my suggestion, because she loves the ocean and happens to live in land-locked central Illinois—but we've also visited family in the Pacific Northwest and will drive up to Wisconsin in the winter to visit other family, despite the difficulty of traveling when she feels so unpredictably ill.

I mean, she's not a saint, of course. We are sisters, so we've known each other a long, long time—there will always be family stories (though admittedly they're mostly stories we tell about our two brothers). She has driven me crazy with worry at times, jumping into owning an equine therapy center without detailed plans, choosing not to take my advice (most often about conserving time, energy, money), getting additional dogs when she already had two (she has four now)... The truth: she has always spent her life profligately, though not shallowly. She hasn't worried much about the future, as I do. She doesn't fear the rainy days or save up for them. Every day is today, now, and demands her full attention.

Funny how a Christian like her can school a Buddhist like me. I believe the human condition is suffering, or at least "discomfort" (depending on your translation), precisely because we are sentient beings aware of time. We cannot help but regret or yearn for the past, and worry or hope for the future. Buddhism seeks to minimize this suffering by encouraging awareness and appreciation of the present. As a Grade A Worrier, I (like my father, the Original Worrier), am drawn to the philosophy of Buddhism because of this.

Oh, of course human beings need a balance: we do need to plan for the future and learn from the past, as well as live in the present. But right now, when I have an unknown amount of time with her, when no one knows how she'll feel at any given time, when that word *cancer* stretches out like a series of dots towards a final period, her way seems like the best way.

She was just down here in Memphis visiting. It may be late August, but it is still hot here, soupy with humidity. After we walked our dogs—slowly—in the neighborhood, we hopped into the backyard pool my husband bought for

$100. The sun seemed to fall slowly through the leaves; hummingbirds visited the nearby feeder, buzzing over our heads. And the two of us—both in our 50s—circled the little pool, threatening to tickle each other's feet. Our giggles pealed like bells over the grass and the Black-Eyed Susans and the wooden fence separating our yard from the neighbors': *ring*, we are here, *ring*, the day is gorgeous, *ring*, we are alive now, despite everything.

Weird

"You're weird," she says.

"You're weirder," I say.

"You're weirdest! I won!" She laughs, a sound that begins with a fake *ho ho ho* and moves into a real chuckle.

"But that can't be true, because you're the queen of weirdness," I say.

"Then you're the empress."

"Your weirdness is bigger than the universe," I say.

"Your weirdness is bigger than the galaxy," she says.

I laugh. "The universe is bigger than the galaxy, silly girl!"

She's giggling on the phone. She knows this, of course, but she likes to get me to tease her. Her dog, Happy, a 120-pound Great Pyrenees, barks in the background. The little dogs begin to bark, too. I hear a door open and close.

"Are you outside?" I ask. "Is someone there?"

"I think it's the next rider," she says. "But L's taking care of this one."

She sounds tired. She is tired. It's late summer, and she'll die in December. She's sorry that she can't work with as many kids as she usually does, talking them through grooming their horse, helping them put on the bridle and saddle, helping them mount. But she's relieved, too, as she literally cannot do as much as she used to, that others are taking up the slack.

I'm wondering how many more times we'll have this conversation, varied over the years but mostly the same. Substitute "I love you" for "you're weird," and you know what we're saying.

The World Is Filled with Bees

The mowers chopped down one of my favorite plants, a multi-stemmed beauty with tiny white flowers the bees and other insects love. And after cursing the men on the machines, my second instinct was to berate myself for being old and out of shape and not mowing my own damn yard. I am only mid-life but I know a little of helplessness and I recognize it in others: how we respond to what happens, how we bow our heads or call people names or shrug our shoulders and go on.

What was lost this time was a bit of bug paradise taking up less than a square foot of garden. I never knew its name so I cannot replace it, only hope the roots live and regenerate. I know my sister would say it will come back, as she buries her dying hands in the black soil of Illinois to plant tomatoes and petunias, fruit and flowers we think she will enjoy this year before the dark takes over more and more of the day. She has always believed and I haven't, and neither has made any difference.

Still the world is filled with bees. Still they seek what sweetness they can find.

The Person We Need

Celebrities die all the time and we mourn what more they could have given to the world. I get songs stuck in my head but if I tell my sister she doesn't know them, willfully ignorant of pop culture. I tease her but I love that she fills her head with other material: old and new human stories, the right environment for different plants, the names of other people's children.

There are so many things I don't understand, including the ways to talk to teenagers in trouble or people who are about to lose a loved one or that dying loved one, things she does without self-consciousness or even much effort. The irony: the person we need now that my sister is dying is my sister.

Who Wants to Live Forever? The rest of the words aren't right but the tune is and that's how I feel when I'm fumbling through, talking to her on the phone now, early in her dying, perhaps a year to go according to the doctors. I'm not always getting the words right but the tone works and she gets that, even as her own tone as she says goodbye every time is too gentle, a hand on my shoulder telling me I'll be okay.

What I Don't Know

1. At what point my mother knew she could no longer make the decision to take her own life and avoid the suffering of the last weeks of cancer. I had always assumed she would. She had spoken of it before, had always said what we could do for animals was a kindness we withheld from humans.

2. Why I sometimes feel lonely when I'm with people, how that glass wall comes down between me and them, a separation as abrupt and painful as a puppy suddenly weaned from its mother.

3. How to prevent or stop that loneliness, to lift the wall, to loosen the strings tying up my vulnerable heart like a roast in the refrigerator, and know that I belong.

4. How my sister could go through nine months of denial as the cancer ravaged her, never facing death or telling others she was dying. She believed in the afterlife; she believed in God. I expected her to tell us not to worry, that she was not afraid. Instead, I think she was hoping for a miracle that never came, not at any of the times in her life that she needed one.

5. When I stopped bringing my blanket to sleepovers, the green one with satiny trim that smelled like my mom. I remember once when I forgot it, sitting in my friend's bedroom—the wealthy friend whose bedroom was bigger than the one I shared with my sister—and sobbing, bereft not only of family but of everything that had ever been good in my life, as if I had been left on a rock in the arctic and my friend and her cigarette-smoking mother and the green shag carpet were nothing but frightening illusions.

6. How she bore it, serving as the little mother to my brother and me when our mom had epilepsy and the drugs kept her in bed. How did she decide what to cook each night for our father and the two of us and herself and my older brother, with a plate brought up to our mom if she could not make it down the stairs to sit at the table? Did she fall exhausted into her twin bed at night, twelve going on forty? Did she swallow down her worry with her childhood? And why did I never ask her?

7. What I should have said when she drove down to visit, six and a half hours in the car, already fatigued and in pain, and she overheard me telling my husband how hard it was to see her suffering. She came to me later and said, *I am so sorry to contribute to your stress. I don't want you to worry about me.* And I said, *Wouldn't you be upset, if I had cancer?*
7a. Except I do know. I should have said, *Thank you for taking care of me, even now.*

The Future I Expected

After Trump was elected, I imagined having to flee the South in the case of a civil war in America. Her horse farm in central Illinois seemed a good place to go; we could grow food there if we needed to, and it was not near any big cities. It seemed like a haven, despite her emotionally abusive husband. And I always assumed we'd be old together, giggling at our great nieces and great nephews' weddings.

Fat

Stress and menopause have made me fat, and there's no mitigation: it circles my abdomen, inviting heart disease and his friends. I lame joke in my head that I'm putting on the pounds my sister has lost to cancer. As if I could truly carry any of the burden of her dying. And every well-meaning relative and gaping mouth of advertising who talks to me about losing just doesn't get it. Loss isn't a gain, ever. Ask the bluebird whose egg never hatches. Ask the hacked milkweed. Skin wants to be whole. Blood loves everything it touches.

She Wanted to Go to the Sea One Last Time

I have been insensitive to delight, too busy avoiding stones in the road to notice Icarus falling from the sky—or before that, his flying. I have stoppered my ears to the singing as I worked out some problem in my head, I have watched others speak and thought only about what I would say. Swimming in the ocean I have seen pelicans coast by on cupped wings and looked over at my sister, her eyes closed in pleasure, and in the midst of sun and breeze and the shifting embrace of salt water I let my throat close with the knowledge of her dying—great gods of the otherworld I almost let her see me weep. I have so much to be forgiven for. I am alive still, and the dog resting her chin in my hand gives me the whole soft weight of her head.

You're Too Late

I had found three outfits that I liked: the same style pants in three colors (navy, tan, and rust), with a pretty and flattering shirt to match each. They were $20 each, so I kept hesitating on whether to buy two or three of the outfits. And then there was an emergency of some kind, and I got a call from my sister saying she had dropped everything and gone home.

I found her stuff on the floor, sorted out the things she was thinking of buying from her purse and sweater. Just when I was carrying them towards my cart, having decided to buy all three outfits, there she was smiling. "I thought you had gone home already," I said.

"No, but now you're too late to come with me," she said.

"Why?" I said, and then I woke up to the cat running back and forth across the room.

Her Funeral

Our father's second wife saying only, "You look so much like her now!" And I know it's because of the weight I gained while she was sick.

Nets

*...something / Is gone lonely / Into the headwaters of
the Minnesota.*

—*James Wright*

She hiccupped and groaned through her last days, the pain a
hook in her abdomen. I don't know what loneliness she had
then, her eyes unseeing, the drugs dribbling from her mouth
though we urged her to swallow them like pure nectar. I hope
she dreamed of the summer, sun and butterflies landing like
blessings on her back. My love couldn't carry her wherever
she had to go. In the other room, her friends talked of anything but death.

Was the end a graceful dive and immersion into
swift-flowing current, suffocation giving way to quicksilver
glints and subtle lights? Where am I supposed to row now,
my boat drifting severed across the waters?

The Dog Park

It's the time of COVID-19, June already. We've been social distancing since mid-March, staying away from restaurants, concerts, friends. My life isn't much different, honestly. I'm at home unless I go for an errand at the drugstore or pet store. With one exception: my husband and I take our dogs to the off-leash dog park daily, often twice.

When friends check in via message or email or videocall, I joke that I've done nothing since the last time we talked. But that's not quite true. The dog park is exercise, outdoor time, and socializing, all in one. We don't chat with other dog owners every time, but we do most times. It's easy to keep six feet between us, we're outside, so we don't wear masks. A small social interaction makes us feel less isolated, makes me feel a little less lonely. It often starts with me saying, "Sorry! She's only nine months old" as Skye, the puppy, jumps on yet another person to get attention. If the person says, "No problem, it's the dog park! I expect to get jumped on," then we have a few minutes chat.

"What's your dog's breed?" I ask.

"Anatolian Shepherd," the red-mustached guy says. "He's six months and eighty pounds."

"Oh my gosh!" I say. (It's the South, so I never say, "oh my god," which offends some people.) "He's going to be a really big boy!"

"The books say maybe 120, 140 pounds," he says.

"Wow. Well, my puppy loves him. They're playing so well together!"

We pause to watch them run and wrestle, well-loved puppies practicing their own social skills.

After, as we continue our walk through the 100-acre off-leash park, my husband and I chat about how cute the puppy was, how nice the owner. Not all owners are nice, and not all dogs are the right playmate for our pup. She has her own ways of deciding whether to play with another dog. Body language, it usually seems to come down to. The same way we know whether to half-run to grab her and put her on the leash—because the person is pushing her away or worse, holding their hands up, which only encourages Skye to jump more.

If there are no other suitable dogs, Skye jumps on our older dog, Duncan, and they run and wrestle, dive to the ground, one on its back, the other on top. They play like they do at home, but across a much greater space. They jump into the ponds—there are at least four in our usual route—and Skye swims, Duncan wades. It's a romp of epic proportions, with plenty of side-excursions for interesting smells. Every once in a while they find something to roll in—usually something long-dead—or something more freshly dead that Skye picks up and uses for a game of keep-away from us.

The sun strengthens, getting hot, or sinks and a breeze comes up. We watch the owners and their dogs coming towards us, or away. We keep a careful watch for children, who Skye overwhelms with her exuberance, and leash her if we see them.

It's peaceful, joyful, often funny. It's the center of my days, the routine that keeps me going. And many, many times, as we drive home, I burst into tears because I miss my sister, I miss her Great Pyrenees Happy, and how he loved the dog park when she was down to visit. I wish she could have known our two goldens, could be walking with us, healthy. I wish for more time with her, I wish she had a different life, with more time and health for these kinds of walks. I want to tell her the dogs we saw, the puppies we patted, as I often did, on the phone, during one of our thrice-daily talks. I want, and I wish, and I miss her, and her absence is a dark howling emptiness.

What Happened

She has died and the world is ending. These two things happen simultaneously, though one did not cause the other. The world ends every day for someone, loss piling on loss until it topples—personal disaster like the closet door you open and everything falls out, burying you. Is it ever funny for the person underneath?

But back to the world as *earth*: ice caps melting, storms carrying soil and lives away as though they're nothing. Nothing being done to stave off any of this, and yet all I can do right now is take pictures of my pets and speak out loud to the dead: *I wish you could see the puppy now, she's bigger and gives wicked side-eye. I wish I had taken you to England. I wish your life had not been so often a slog through other people's anger.*

Some memories are so sharp there is no safe way to handle them. I cannot even give them away, my hands too tender to hold them, my hands filled like water balloons with our blood, Sister. Sister, nothing is actually funny anymore, my laugh a dull single thud like what you hear from another room and stand up, reluctantly, your joints creaking, to see what has happened.

Sister, I don't know what my life means without you to tell what happened.

Eater of Fishes

Surviving sister, which means left behind, lost child in a public space, crowds milling indifferently about their business like upright ants and no one is coming back to find her. I mean me. If it's not a brag for the dead it's a beg for sympathy—poor blade of grass pulled apart by some mysterious hand, snail shell curled empty under the flowerpot. I could tell you she was a quiet spring rain, not a super-nova, that she made violets bloom, that they came up through her skin, that she was a meadow, that it was not possible to be lonely when she laughed. That one of the last things she said was *Don't forget K is a vegetarian when you set out the leftovers.* That I'm not, I'm a pescatarian, an eater of fishes. That it wasn't surprising she was laying out the table for us one last time.

Lame

I want to write letters to her, to tell her the things I wish I could tell her on the phone, but I can't. I simply can't. No letter meant for others to read could possibly be authentic. What would I say to her, "Dear Weirdy" or more likely just "Weirdy, the puppy is so much more fun now that she's less bitey. But I severely bruised my knee trying to step over the puppy gate and I can't walk her or play rough with her right now, so she goes off to doggy daycare every day. I get up to spend a few minutes with her in the morning, and see her after Andy picks her up in the early evening. It's like sending a toddler off to school; I can now imagine how parents feel." And what would she say? That the puppy loves me, and this won't inhibit our bonding. That I need to take care of myself. That everything will be okay, and three weeks isn't that long.

Talking on the phone

My husband calls me when he's driving home from work.
We chitchat about our days, sharing the details that would
bore anyone else: the kitten cuddled with me on the couch
for a half hour, there was a Rose-breasted Grosbeak at the
bird feeder, I talked to my friends on Zoom. He used to ask
me, every day, if I'd spoken with my sister and if anything
interesting was going on in her world. I had nearly always
spoken with her. She told me about her husband admitting
how furious he was after her latest car accident, when instead
of asking if she was okay, he yelled at her. She told me about
her dogs, her horses, her job as a hospital chaplain. She asked
about my state of mind, the peaks and valleys of my moods.
We planned visits and remembered our childhood.
I am so fucking lonely now that I don't have her life in my
life. I am so lonely and it will never be different. How do
people live with this loneliness?

Hypergraphia

The internet talks about people who suffer from hypergraphia, the affliction causing them to write compulsively. My friend says she had it after her father died, but she doesn't say whether it was bane or balm. Until you are in it, swimming in the muck of grief, you don't know what you might do: push your hands against the top of your legs as I did after our mother died, over and over; sleep eighteen hours a day; bake as if you had a whole church bake sale to supply by yourself. Grief can scissor through you until you don't recognize your own cut and misplaced pieces. I hung her Christmas stocking this year, but I have not yet gone through old photo albums to watch us being young together. I think she asked her friends to check up on me, because I get random texts with raw words trying to comfort. My own words ooze out of me like mud. I don't want to be with people—my irritation a mosquito only I can hear—and I don't want to be alone. I am restless to move, shout, punch—and I ache in all my bones, fall breathless when talking, my lungs heaving. Can't I just sleep for a few months, let my body adjust to this new condition while my mind rests? She must have been so tired, having to write her own ending like that.

Litany of Monday

A purebred cat hunts the birds at my backyard feeder. I fear it is homeless. My knee hurts, an ache like aging and slick mud. She died six weeks ago. It feels like longer. It feels like she is still dying. The light through the window is gray. My hair, undyed, would be gray. Gray is not the color of sadness. It is the color of numb. Numb, dumb, limb, stump. Would a sharp slap knock me out of this sinking? Yesterday the frogs were singing. Today the bluebirds chase each other off the frozen birdbath. I can neither chase the cat away, nor catch and help it, hobbled as I am in my knee corset. My sister had a bad knee for twenty years or more. I wanted her to get a replacement, but she could not stand the thought of machinery inside her body, something alien that did not belong. She died of cancer. The birds are jewels of color or camouflage, small perfect machines of flight. If I could not love animals, I would disappear.

Mind Like the Sky

I'm looking for the flash point of the mind, where my thoughts' vapor ignites and burns away—just for a moment— so I can find peace. It lasts that briefly, flame-like and cleansing, and sometimes an hour of stillness does not bring it, like six hours of driving barely brings me home, or at least back to where home once was, in the middle of the middle of the country, far from cities and flat as hell, according to my father, who grew up in the hills of Pennsylvania and was the first person to introduce me to meditation. I drove those hours monthly when she was sick, chewing gum and drinking iced tea to stay awake, still resisting the machine to help me breathe when I was asleep, so ugly and unromantic. Her dying surrounded by the cornfields didn't blowtorch my monkey mind though it was winter and loss bit cold at my fingers. During her illness it was all jumbled blocks of time and worry and text messages between those of us who loved her. She never wrote a will. She never talked about her death. Sometimes she was the most enlightened person I had ever met, sometimes the least. I don't know what I expect—mind like a coffin, mind like the sky.

Toad

I'm in that stage of grieving where the hurt affects every-thing, permeates everything, but it's not acute. It's like that ache in your stomach that could be hunger, could be just the usual overproduction of acid, could be a pre-symptom of a cold—you're just not sure. Only that it makes you slow and dull, stolid as a toad.

Blue Jay

I hope the Blue Jay didn't need the two feathers it left in our back yard, blue and black striped with white tips. I hope it lifted off easily into a sky safer than the rest of this troubled world where actual human beings torture and kill others out of rage and sickness and politics. It doesn't start with frat boys yelling inebriated words across campus to proclaim their supremacy, but that is one of the steps. I didn't think the word *fear* when I was an undergrad in sneakers and pleated jeans, but I never walked past Greek Row by myself at night. Even then I dreamt of flight, a return to the gravel driveway leading to an aluminum-sided barn where horses waited patiently in the fragrant dust to carry me out into the fields. My brothers remind me how much work it all was, the barn and the horses, the hay and the manure. They want me to say it wasn't paradise. It was more complex than that—our father's rage, our mother's illness—but I always thought if I could go back as an adult I could make it perfect. I suppose I thought one day I might retire there, or someplace like it, with my sister, and we would grow old and happy. Even when we no longer rode, the horses would greet us over the gate, sweet grass hanging from their mouths as they chewed. But now she has flown on ahead, always the first of us, the bravest. If there is another life, she's found it. I wonder if what happens to some men is the loss of hope. If the Blue Jay is already falling from the sky then what use is tenderness?

Technology

Ten days after her death, she "liked" something I had posted on social media. Clearly her technologically challenged husband had been on her computer and forgotten he was logged into her account. I knew that immediately, but still it was a shock: her name suddenly appearing on the screen, visible not only to me but to my other friends. What did they think? No one said anything, and eventually her name got lost in the ether.

B Calls

B, my sister's friend from Colorado, calls. They met at a Mennonite church, when B felt called to stop in, though she'd never been to a Mennonite church before. My sister was working on committees designed to help people, social justice work focusing on immigrants. They both believed in the tangible nature of faith, that God guided them to do things. They both believed in alternative health therapies and the broad nature of spirituality, how other faiths got a lot of things right, how Native American traditions carried wisdom and the rituals of other cultures healed.

"I was just thinking of you," I say when I answer the phone.

"I knew you were!" she says. "A dragonfly came into my room and flew around me, a big one, the size of my hand, and I said, 'Okay, okay, I'll call her!'"

B came to Illinois for a month the summer before my sister died, spending early mornings in the clover meadow with her, meditating and praying, watching the dragonflies and the butterflies moving across the purple and white flowers.

"So she's bossy even now, huh?" I say.

"Exactly," B laughs. "So how are you?"

I am a writer, a poet. I say things with words precisely, trying always to get past the surface into the heart. But on the phone, I can be inarticulate. "I miss her so much," I blurt. "She would have been so good to talk to about this auto-immune disease I maybe have. She would have had such good ideas. She would have listened."

"Sister, I know," B says. She can say this because she also spent the last week of my sister's life with her, with us. We would never have made it through without B. B stayed calm as she deteriorated, moved swiftly through the last phase. She was bridge and buffer between my sister's husband and the rest of us, staying at the farmhouse, offering him the same calm and compassion she gave to us all when we couldn't spare anything for him. She talked to the hospice nurses when his reason broke down, when he didn't seem to understand what was happening. She administered medicine and held my sister's hand and talked to her as though she was sure her old friend was listening.

"I feel her so strongly with me now, when I set up a meditation, when I wonder what I should do next," B says.

"Her friend just sent me the quilt she made out of ribbons from horse shows that she and our mom won," I say.

"That's amazing!" she says. "I have her butterfly shoes. I carried them in my car for months, just put them on my little altar for today's meditation."

What You Deserve

You died at fifty-eight. You didn't get to fly enough, never came to England with me, had few days free of worry over bills. Or rather, the rest of us worried for you, and you just went on, day after day, walking the corridors of the hospital in your aqua skirts and pink hats to keep out the fluorescent light, sitting with patients and their families while the bad news came down and pressed onto their shoulders.

Oh, I wished so many things different for you: a sweet husband without a temper, a child for you to love, money to keep the farm going so troubled kids could come and ride the horses. A thin body, because our mother and grandmother taught you that was important. A house cleaner, because you were so busy visiting people in need that the dog hair and dirt and dust and dishes piled up and up until it was hard to visit you.

When our beloved cat died under the wheels of our own car you drove six hours to comfort us, arrived to find us nearly numb. That was only three months before you died, the cancer making you weak as a moth in daytime.

Damn it, Sister, I still wish you'd gotten everything you wanted in life. If I'm furious, that's why. Not that you had to leave me, the phone unringing every day, unalive without your voice. You deserved more. And that God you loved had better welcome you with everything you ever wanted, His hands full with them, offering you wholeness and the peace of a summer horseback ride, tiger lilies trumpeting their color beside the blacktop and honeysuckle singing its sweet angelic scent.

The Woman Walking with a Book

A woman is walking on the sidewalk holding a book. She is building a space in the air to move through, to move in, a series of flat stones in the stream that she walks oblivious. Perhaps she is in need of time, perhaps her house is full of the tensions of living with others—someone watching the news all day now that we have a global pandemic to worry about, which makes us feel more alive and less certain for the first time in far too long, someone else closed in her room sleeping or texting or singing along to stupid videos or talking a friend through a difficult romance, the same things we did so long ago except it was handwriting in a journal and records spinning on the player in the living room so everyone heard our sugary music, and the telephone cord stretched around a corner for the veneer of privacy.

Now that we are alone in our houses because we are trying so hard not to throw or catch a disease no one seems to know enough about, is anyone yearning for those old days? I know without the virtual rooms in which my friends talk about poetry I would be so much lonelier, even if in normal times I get lonelier the more time I spend online. But I am also the one who asked my sister's doctor the prognosis, when her husband and I stood beside her seated on the examining table. He never said *terminal*, but I knew, and I wanted to know everything: dates and stages, what to expect. She never admitted to dying, as if by saying it she invited death inside. One of the tabs open on my computer shows the numbers: how many confirmed cases worldwide, how many dead. At the top of the page flicker advertisements for shoes, mortgage loans. I suppose this is what passes for optimism now.

Now that I can't ask my sister, I want to go out and find the woman with the book, surely walking the sidewalks of my neighborhood even now, and ask what she thinks while we stand the mandated six feet apart and try to keep ourselves alive.

Gratitude

It is hard to be grateful for much with you gone. Even to address you as "Sister" isn't quite right, though neither is your name. We wrote to each other "Weirdy" and "Crazy Girl" and all manner of nickname, so much more intimate than given names and full to the throat with history and love. I'm not sure anymore what I should call you, now that you belong to the universe.

The puppy you told me to go ahead and get is sitting outside in the rare sunshine of January, and I am grateful for her. No sun is without echoes of you, your skin a rich red-brown instead of burned like mine. Not much is without echoes of you, diagnosed in March and gone in December, on your way perhaps to do more important things, though I was never as sure as you. I should focus on life and not afterlife anyway, the sunshine and the daffodils six inches up already here in what they call the mid-South, the key lime pie I ate mid-morning left over from a weekend's dinner with friends.

Much of what I would be grateful for is double edged: you at the beach that last time, free from pain only when you were immersed in the sea; that your husband spent your last nine months finally curbing his anger; that my bruised knee will heal and I will walk again those places we loved, passing the memory of you going slow, all that your lungs could handle, like passing through a ghost filled with light, brightness clinging to my sleeve like dust as I go on without you into the fading afternoon.

Bodies

How does a body define a person? It is just a body, and the ones we have are all so different: wide, narrow, tall, short, long-haired, stiff in one knee, tending to skip, gliding, fleshy in the arms... What I really mean to say is that I don't understand how a person is her body, how my sister's body is gone and that means so is she. She was more than her body. She was a voice on the phone, a generosity in the world, an intelligence bent on intuition. She listened. I suppose you must do those things with your body.

It was because of her body that the doctors missed the cancer for a year, ignoring the symptoms. One told her everything would be okay if she went on a keto diet. She had been losing weight without trying, throwing up at random, having stomach pain. Our mother died of pancreatic cancer. But my sister's body was overweight, which is paradoxically less important, less visible.

She died only nine months after diagnosis. Cancer in the lungs, bones, and abdomen. It was the abdominal cancer that killed her, and that was the type they never biopsied. Even after treatment began, doctors said her pain and nausea must be due to the chemo.

In her last two days, she was unresponsive—except when she got the hiccups. Then, after every hiccup, she made a little sound between a groan and a cry. They hurt. Her abdomen hurt. Despite all the pain and sedating medications, she hurt.

There is so much to be angry about.

I still have to live in/with my body. And it is bigger than ever, swelled by the food I couldn't stop pushing into my mouth while my sister ate less and less. As if I could eat for her. As if, by eating, I could negate how painful the act was for her, how she didn't know when she might throw up even the most innocuous foods. Or maybe I ate because I was trying to drown the anxiety and the fear of grief, the reality of my sister's suffering. Or maybe I ate for something to do while doctors bungled her treatment and she listened to their encouraging updates—the cancer in the lungs is visibly shrinking!—instead of to the news of her body, which was starving itself and pummeling her with pain. Maybe I ate because she floated along in denial, not writing a will or making plans for end-of-life care or even talking about what type of service she wanted, despite being a pastor herself.

Anyway I am stuck in my body, which also has decided to hurt in new ways. Some pain is expected: feet and legs a little more stressed by the greater weight they must carry. But my hands hurt, too. Am I developing arthritis? What, if anything, should I do about it? Or is it psychological, pain I must hold like I hold my grief, like an overfilled bowl of soup I am trying not to spill?

Anyway the world is without my sister, who was many things but always a caregiver. She was a chaplain at the hospital where she spent most of her last month as a patient. Wearing bright colors—aqua and pink were her favorite— and a sun hat to keep the fluorescent lights out of her eyes, she walked the halls of that hospital, sharing her presence with patients. She never insisted on prayer or a particular type of religion, but offered to help carry the burden for a little while. I could not do that, to come upon strangers in a time of vulnerability and uncertainty and ask the right questions, be sparing with answers, leave them feeling understood and comforted. For her it was effortless, as natural as sleep.

Because she has no body anymore to form words and push air out over vocal cords, I don't know what she would say to me now. She might well tell me not to write about her, not to think too much about what I have lost, the things I did or did not do for her. She would likely say it's not worth being angry at the doctors, at her, at a thin-worshipping culture, at the body/mind/soul question, at much of anything else. I hope she would say *I love you* and *don't forget* and *I no longer hurt*. I hope she would say *don't worry, my heaven is real*.

Peach Crisp

I make peach crisp—fresh ripe peaches, butter, brown sugar, oatmeal, flour, cinnamon—and she says *Why didn't you ever make peach crisp when I was there?* It's the same faux-outraged tone she had whenever I made cake or chocolate-chip cookies when we just lived in different states, but actually I don't think I ever made peach crisp before in my life. And peaches were her favorite fruit. Why didn't I make it for her? It's so good, rendering average peaches into gooey heaven, topped with a cookie-like crumble the flavor of childhood Sunday afternoons.

For that matter, why didn't I take her to England, sit with her in manicured church gardens, serve her afternoon tea with little sandwiches and scones and pastries? Why didn't we swim more, water baby that she was, moving fluidly from one broken person to the next, offering them her presence? And why didn't we find out about the cancer earlier, when she had still been well enough to do everything she loved, when I could have made a traveling carnival of board games and beaches for her to rule as a benevolent, giggling queen? I would have gone into debt for her, sold off my body parts to be claimed after her death when I would be no use to anyone for months and months. By the time they handed her a diagnosis it rattled like a gourd, filled with the days she had left.

All I can do for her now is remember a dark-haired girl biting into her life—the only one she had, and hers alone—trying hard to taste it all before it was gone.

But I Would Not Give Up This Burden

I carry her bones in my bones, her pain in my nerves, the distant sound of the ocean in my ears. After she died, I smashed my right knee and now I mirror the twisted moves she made after her popped ligament on the softball field all those years ago. Always calm in pain, she told us when her cancer-hollowed bones ached in the same way you might announce you'd like water with dinner.

I carry her heart in my body but I am not yet ready to listen to its tales. I can only bear to tell my own tales about her, and I knew more than most. *Once upon a time, a curly-haired laughing girl walked a garden maze with no exit. She helped anyone she came across, picking apples for the rat-people and brushing burrs from the horse-people's manes. They all loved her but sometimes when the dark came they let her struggle on alone. And then she left, and no one knew what to do.*

My tales don't always omit her specific suffering: the children she never had, the carousel of rejection. I carry her voice in my throat but I cannot speak all her truths, or all her lies. I carry my grief in my hands and they mostly do what is needed but oh, they ache.

Indigo Bunting

She told me she and our grandfather saw a bright turquoise bird, brighter than the Navajo bracelets we inherited from our grandmother on the other side, a bird so bright it almost stunned them. After much searching in antique hand-drawn bird books, they decided it was an Indigo Bunting. So when my friend mentions Indigo Buntings during a video call, I make a note to buy thistle seed, move the feeder farther from the house. Her favorite color was turquoise, and light peach, and seafoam. She was a bright thing in the halls of the hospital where she worked as a chaplain, listening to the necessary stories. I want her to exist now in museums of splashy paintings surrounded by gardens of blooming daisies, peonies, tulips—colors beyond human description. I wish I had taken her to more gardens, indebted myself ten times over to fly with her to Hawaii—Plumeria!—and England where every church has fountains of orange Crocosmia. Yesterday my dog scared an Indigo Bunting bathing in the dust on the path at the dog park. After it flew off, I looked and looked for it in vain.

Relearning

Have you ever taken off a bandage—one that had been covering the tip of your thumb—and had to re-learn how to use that essential digit, the one we say keeps the thumbless from taking over? I imagine it would be like that, if she was suddenly alive again. First, I would fall on my knees and beg forgiveness for not doing everything she wanted in this world. And then we would do it.

Slipped

In college I spent the night kissing and talking with a boy, and when he woke from dozing he asked, *Why aren't you asleep?* I said, *I don't want to miss anything.* I wish I still lived like that, anticipation spiking through my veins, instead of falling time and again into smothering shame.

A friend once told me my picture was next to *well-adjusted* in the dictionary and I thought *yes*, I thought I was doing such a good job, I didn't even admit it felt like acting, I thought everyone's life was at least a bit of acting. You decided how to be and tried your best: wasn't that right?

I only knew then I didn't want to be like my sister with her outsized moods and demands that the world be different—she made our parents' worry bloom and I was taught that was the worst a daughter could do. As I got older I felt small things too much, my past control slipping, slipped, so each new hurt was multiplied by previous wounds. By the time my sister died, she could not believe how tender I was.

Now I press my face into the loss of her, I cannot help it, I don't know how I lost the knack but my nightmares are about forgetting all my lines, or never having known them.

The Best Things People Said to Me After She Died

1. I will check in on you, asking you specifically how you are doing in terms of your grief. I will do this on a regular basis (once a week, once a month) for as long as you need it. I will even set a reminder on my phone to do it. If you don't want to talk about it, just tell me.

2. I understand that all your griefs are connected, so you will grieve your mother, your pets, your first marriage, your career, the horse farm where you grew up, and all your other losses extra hard during this time.

3. You can tell me as often as you need to, in as much detail as you wish, about your grief. I will not feel burdened. It matters that you cried in the car on the way back from the dog park. I cannot offer any solutions, but I will listen.

4. When someone dies who has known you your whole life, it may feel like part of your identity has died. I will listen to your old stories, the details of your life and your life with her: how you fake-fought about who would get your cocker spaniel, Amber, on your bed every night when you shared a room; how she used to talk as she was falling asleep, making less and less sense.

5. Your life has meaning, even without your connection to her. Your presence in the world is different from hers, but just as important. She may have helped hundreds of people by being with them during hard times, working with them at her therapeutic riding center, and visiting them as a nurse or chaplain, but every life has ripples that are not always easy to see.

6. There is no timeline for grief, or for joy. You may feel both within the same minute. Ordering a gardenia bush—your one exception to choosing native plants these days—may bring delight and also hollowness, because she will never see it, never smell its heavy fragrance that your mother, she, and you love.

7. Missing the stupid things—the ritual exchange of "you're weird," the pet medical advice when you know you're going to the vet anyway, making chocolate chip cookies just the way she liked them—is normal.

8. Write as many words about her, and your loss of her, as you wish. Maybe people will eventually read them; maybe not. It doesn't matter. Write them anyway. Write thousands. It's not selfish, and even if it is, that's okay. You don't get a prize for "best bereaved person."

9. It will get better. It will never go away, this loss, this emptiness, this ache, but it will be less intrusive. Eventually you won't cry every day. Eventually you won't reach for your phone to call her. Eventually you won't think of every vacation in terms of whether she would like it: beach or mountains, warm or cold, cathedral or moors.

10. Keep talking about her. Don't be afraid of your own pain, or causing it in others. She did not disappear out of your memories. Anyone who ever heard her giggle will never forget it. She was here. She was real. She still is.

Everything Will Be All Right

I woke from a dream in which I could see the dead. They were as real as the living. My sister sat beside me, her arms around me. She smelled like roses and hay. She said, *Everything will be all right*. She spoke in her gentlest voice, the voice she used when she called me at work twenty years ago to tell me my sweet red dog, Mick, had died. The specialist vet had taken him in for an MRI and he had gone into arrest and they had to know that minute if they should keep trying to revive him. They had called and she had made the decision. She had spared me that. She had loved me that much. She always had.

In the dream, she held me and said everything would be all right.

Obituary

She was a pastor at Lake Fork United Church of Christ in Atwood, a chaplain at OSF Hospital in Champaign, and co-founder of Healing Horse Stables, an equine therapy center in Pesotum. A long-term member of Westminster Presbyterian Church, the Disciples of Christ Community Church, and the interfaith Sisters in Faith, she became an ordained minister towards the end of a life that was always dedicated to service. Her jobs—paid and volunteer—included chaplain at Kemmerer Village, home health nurse, international peace missionary in South America, nurse at the Spanish Catholic Center in the D.C. area, hospice volunteer, nurse educator for pregnant teens, immigrant advocate, and equine-assisted therapist. She particularly enjoyed working with troubled teenagers, and pastoral care. Beloved by many communities, she reached out to people in need of help. Her natural gifts of spiritual and emotional presence, wisdom, and joyfulness made a profound difference in many lives. Towards the end, when she was not speaking much, she still said, "I love you" in response to visitors, and that is her legacy: a great love for all.

What would she say?

I don't know where the energy of you is, the spirit or the mind or the atoms or the intelligence. I hope you have something to do, because even when you were exhausted and wrung out emotionally you couldn't sit still for long.

Every time I can't tell you something, it hurts. I want to tell you about this amped-up fatigue and pain, to hear your sympathy, to know you love me without judgment, to know for absolute certain that you don't think I'm whining. To hear you say just the right thing, effortlessly. To find myself able to appreciate my other friends, even when they say the wrong things—*But you don't look tired! Are you finding it hard to think about other things besides your symptoms? I get tired too—I haven't gone to the gym in days.*

And now you are asking me, *What would I say?*

You would say *You do a lot, and people don't love you because of how well you clean the house or weed the garden.* You would say *Maybe some ice cream is in order.* You would say *Don't forget to cuddle your pups.* You would say *I love you, little Weirdy.*

Curse hot flashes and tears tumbling out like confetti, getting everywhere. Curse numbers, counting up the days since my sister's death. Curse her death, too painful, too fast. Curse suffering of all kinds: the detainee dead in custody, and the dog hit by a car. Curse the politicians who build the laws about cages, curse the mouths speaking hate. Curse fate or bad luck, cancer, virus like an exploding sun. Curse the rock in your shoe, the ugly slide into age, the bum knee, the bad back. Curse fathers' anger. Curse clichés, especially those about bright sides and it could be worse. Curse remembering. Curse the hurts we can laugh about and the ones we can't. Curse the disappearance of birds, the disappearance of who and what we love, popping out of existence like 1970s special effects. Curse entropy. Curse until you have no breath, curse breathlessness, and when you're done, get up and try to love what's left.

Pieces of my sister ride the currents of my house, caught and spinning sometimes in unexpected eddies. She hid when someone lifted a camera or, later, a phone, to take a photo of her, and her teeth clicked shut—how dare we document the body she bore, always too full for her own approval or the world's? How could we betray her by capturing her face, the pinch of fat under the chin, the wild curly brown hair reaching for something invisible, and the blue, blue eyes I hope always to see when I command my brain to remember? Still I know her in the painting she loved of a kingfisher diving—her blue-green skirt, the flash of her face as she stepped through a numbered doorway to sit with a stranger engulfed in foam-white hospital sheets. And when my elbow skims the quilt our friend made from ribbons won at horse shows in the 1970s, the scent of oiled leather and horse sweat rises in the hallway. I see my sister atop her bay mare Lady, asking for a trot with little more than a slight forward lean, the two of them buffed and shined for the show ring.

Once I called her for a recipe for crab cakes, and though she never wrote anything down, she guessed for me, and I scribbled on a glossy page pulled from a magazine. Somehow now the sound of crab cakes frying in a cast iron pan is the sound of her voice when I came to her after my marriage broke and confessed I was not sure I deserved to live. *Stay*, I hear, and the sizzle becomes the edge of a wave popping and bubbling on the sand. *Stay* is the only word I remember but she held my wrist and made me believe I was her beacon in the rough, dark sea when she was mine, she was always mine.

Dear Sister,

I believe in the practice of gratitude, have seen the articles showing measurable improvement in mood and cognition—I just find it difficult to engage in the good practices of self-care when I'm so deeply shaken. Though our brothers are still left, it feels like you were the last person who had known me all my life. No, that's not quite right: you were one of two people who cared about the minutiae of my life, who I told things that I hadn't carefully selected for their interest or relevance to the conversation. The other person, of course, is my husband, for whom I am grateful every day because of his cheer, his wit, his love for animals, for how he asked me when you were alive if I'd heard from you that day, for how he asks me now how I am "in myself," a Britishism I love. So: I am grateful we took you to the beach less than two months before you died, how you managed to get into the ocean every day we were there despite having so much stomach pain that you hardly ate. I am grateful you loved my stepdaughter and made her know it, that she could come along on that beach trip. I thought I was good with college kids but you were alight with laughter, your face like open arms, then as always.

I am grateful for the puppy you encouraged me to get. She grows redder every day, her gold transmuting towards chestnut, like the horses you and I each loved when we were growing up: your Royal, small and willing, and my Crest, a big boy who took care of me as though he knew nothing else (though we both know he made adult riders work for any semblance of control). I am grateful that we managed to get you down to meet the puppy while you still could, your friend driving you halfway and me picking you up, you handling the seven hours in the car as best you could. I wish the pup hadn't been in her puppy-biting stage; she is so much more fun now, her retriever mouth softer, gentler, and able to calm down for cuddling.

(I am trying to leave out what I am still angry about, the incompetence of doctors and your husband's anger. I am grateful that he found a way to curb that anger in your final nine months, but why couldn't he have done that years earlier?)

Still, it is sunny out, here in late January in Tennessee, and the daffodils are six inches up, which means they'll bloom in a couple of weeks. A Downy Woodpecker eats at the suet feeder. I don't live in the windswept center of Illinois like you did, but I have some beauty around me, and that is worth my gratitude.

I'm grateful that my knee will recover in another week or two so I can again walk the puppy, watch her joy and feel the kick and swing of legs moving as they should. I'm grateful that I didn't break my kneecap when I fell, trying to step over the puppy gate. I'm grateful that we have insurance so I could go to the doctor, get the proper knee brace and reassurance and advice. I'm aware of the coincidence of it, that you had a bad knee for so many years and I hurt mine mere weeks after you were gone.

Mostly I'm grateful that we had fifty-one years together, though I expected more. Your giggle was something no one who heard it could ignore, a bell, a trumpet proclaiming that many things might be wrong with the world but there was delight anyway. You set standards I could not reach, older sister, saving the world in rural and urban America, Guatemala, Colombia. You did so by talking with people, offering the gift of your attention and understanding. People who spoke other languages loved you, coming to you through fog and dark to find welcome. And the traumatized children and teens, survivors of violence and abuse, of the mental illness of their caretakers and themselves—you didn't need to know what had happened to them. You gave, and gave, and gave, and you didn't think it was anything, just being yourself.

Okay, so I admit I'm also grateful that I'm not worrying about you every day, about whether you'll be able to pay your bills or whether you'll have another car accident, another head injury. About your angry husband and whether I could ever save you so you might have a true love, be cherished as you deserved. I'm grateful you were never destitute, or homeless, that you managed to always be able to eat and feed your dogs and horses and have heating and air conditioning, despite doing jobs that paid so little. I'm grateful to the people who helped when you needed it, their money and time like flotation cushions in water that sometimes got a little too deep.

Sister, I'm grateful you were alive.

Island dream

I'm on a small island just off the coast of somewhere warm. The island is barely big enough for an open-air house with lofts for sleeping and canoes for going to the mainland. The sea breaks and whispers across the sand. My sister bobs and floats in the water, but I can't tell if she's coming in to shore or swimming out into the turquoise waves.

Two Endings

The raccoon came so often she earned a name: Rachel, for the alliteration, and because she was clearly a female nursing babies. Though at first she scavenged under the bird feeders, soon my husband was setting out seeds and nuts and sometimes watermelon just for her. Plenty smart, she learned he was her benefactor and approached when she spotted him out at dusk. Then she brought her kits, three scampering bandits who photographed well.

Growing up on a horse farm in central Illinois, none of us were surprised when our oldest brother brought home an orphaned raccoon kit, a ball of patterned fur who climbed the back of my sister's chair to steal her peanut butter and jelly sandwich, then ran away, chittering, to her den under the stairs. Eventually, the raccoon was moved out to the barn, and after a year she took herself off into the fields, following the call of a boy raccoon, our mother always said.

At fifty-eight, my sister was diagnosed with cancer in March and died in December. Somewhere in there my husband and I got two big dogs and stopped feeding the raccoons for their own safety. But it is April again and Rachel is back, engorged with milk, her hand-like paws grasping the windowsill. The dogs bark but then seem fascinated by her calm. She presses her nose to the glass on the outside; the dogs press back from the inside.

And for a moment I am standing outside her house, a struggling equine therapy center less than an hour's drive from where we grew up. She is still alive, but her eyes are closed and she is no longer talking, not even in the surprising, unconnected way she used to talk in her sleep, a habit that came back as the opioids pooled in her brain. No one knows how much longer she will live, though one friend said her grandmother held on for two weeks this way—a suffering

I do not wish for my sister, or those of us who love her. The pain still seems to run through her veins, cells whispering to cells like prisoners in the dark, and that makes my own muscles clench and twist, my heart beat staccato. I have to get away, so I plan to drive thirty minutes into town to get some lunch, to swallow my fear and grief with fries and ketchup.

Rachel peers in through the window, hungry, remembering the bounty of food last year. The two dogs turn their golden smiles up to me, but I can see their teeth, their stiffly wagging tails. Guilt curls heavy in my stomach—will she suffer? will her kits suffer?—but I can't feed her. I must abandon her to her own journey, her own wits and instincts in this wooded Tennessee suburb.

When I left the living room, the only place in the old farmhouse with space for the hospital bed, I told my sister I loved her and that I would be back, and I touched her hand. Outside, I sway, growing colder in the raw wind, undecided. I put my hand on the doorknob. Then I turn and cross the gravel path to my car.

The Country of After-Grief

It's Easter, and my remaining family resurrects the old tales: one brother always making the ugliest egg by dipping it in all the colors, our mother hiding an egg behind a book where our father would find it months later. My sister wore bright clothes, even a pastel stole when she became a minister, and the eggs she dyed were delicate turquoise and peach and lavender, mottled like sunset clouds.

We don't talk about her, carefully, the memory brittle as those shells drained and painted with tiny brushes. Messages and photos fly through the ether and my brothers look ahead, their hair gray as mine should be. Don't you miss her? I want to ask them. Do you hurt? But their insides are opaque to me, reported only sporadically by their wives like letters home from the front. I can guess but I don't like to, I know them too well, how they worried for so long they would be the ones cleaning up her mess—bankruptcy, foreclosure, driver's license revoked, things that never happened but could have. She was the child they never signed up to parent, flower child born too late, capable of comforting the poor and wounded but unable to face bills or budgets or retirement plans.

As it turned out she never needed to live for the future. Eldest sibling, always first, still in her fifties. Her absence a hole everything else is drawn through, towards some other place I hope exists, even if it's just the country of after-grief. Frayed, I want to make it there. No stone rolled away, no unbelievable return. Just a place where the hard landscape softens slowly to green under a whisper of rain.

Introduction to Her Collected Sermons

She didn't especially like to preach. Not because she had nothing to say, as you'll see here, but because she didn't relish being the center of attention. She felt that God moved through her in quieter ways, in listening to people in distress, offering a much-needed hug, helping people to find strength in themselves, supporting them in difficult times and celebrating with them as they experienced their triumphs. But of course it was this other-oriented approach to her faith that suffused her sermons with meaning and power. She helped connect listeners with God and with each other, reminding them of the ways they could love each other with the strength and generosity of God's love for them. She reminded people that we are all in this together, so we need to help each other, to give and not to judge. She interwove the themes of love and joy and connection, showing listeners ways to be and understand their better selves. And she did this with the kind of skilled writing that does not proclaim itself but moves fluidly from scholarly insight to personal stories. In this collection you'll get a little bit of her, the nuanced and subtle workings of her mind, the warmth and openness of her heart. Enjoy, and feel renewed.

—K.R.

Mud boots

Today I slipped my feet into the rubber boots you liked—the ones with horses on them—and tromped out into the soggy backyard to fill the bird feeders. The tube feeder was nearly empty despite my having filled it the day before yesterday; we have an irruption of Pine Siskins this year, and they're cleaning us out. Penny looks out the window and chatters at them, smaller than sparrows, streaked dark brown and white with occasional yellow. I refilled the platform feeders too, because the cardinals, chickadees, juncos, wrens, and bluebirds often don't get to eat their fill before it's all emptied by those flocks of Siskins.

And then, though it was forty and overcast, I was enjoying being outside for the second time on this first day of January—the first was the dogs' walk at the off-leash park your Great Pyrenees Happy enjoyed so much—so I wandered around a bit, cleaning up after the dogs, checking on my tiny viburnum and slightly larger dogwood. When my boots sank into the mud and made a sucking sound, you were suddenly with me. We were doing my patrol of the yard together, chatting about spring and gardens, about the daffodils already two inches up in places. You had energy and strength enough to walk with me, teasing me about mud and boots and my stubborn nature.

You were three, you said. *Mom and I were in the barn and you were playing outside. We heard the most awful screams!*

I had a problem, I said. *But I saw a solution.*

We ran out to save you, you said, *only to discover that you had walked out of your boots, which were stuck in the mud. You stood in your sock feet, mud up to your knees, perfectly content.*

I didn't want to wait, I said, though I don't remember, only know this story from my family's retellings. *Maybe I didn't want to bother you.*

Stubborn girl!

Determined, I said.

And then you were gone, and I was wiping my boots on the rug just inside the back door, putting them back inside the storage stool so the dogs wouldn't chew them up.

Grief Uninvented

sister   we walk a forest path   snow falls like a lullaby
ancient trees draw breath into themselves   an owl blinks
from a dark   opening   warm in his mottled cloak   we
know how far   we still have to go   it is nothing   we
are together   pines drop spent needles   to cushion
our steps   this is not a dream   this is something else
something   like a dawn   ancestral   bone memory
sister   it is quiet as living fur under fingertips   you wear
a blue scarf knitted with stars   when we arrive   the
horses will lean down   and blow softly into our faces   at
last we will be born   at last

Ordering a Zero Gravity Chair Online

So much goes on in the country of my backyard that I need a throne to oversee it all. Of course the dogs spill out through the back door into their favorite room. They squat and sniff, chase toads, watch the neighbor's border collie spring up to try to see them over the fence. Finches inhabit the air and the trees, call dibs on the feeder, flee when the mourning doves or the starlings come bumbling in like those old chubby planes barely making the runway. Hummingbirds ignore us all, distant as ballerinas. The lilies I inherited from the previous owner swell, about to open gaudy orange umbrellas that will split and bend backward like curious octopi. Coreopsis presents buttons of green buds in preparation for a festival of yellow.

I should be planting new flowers for the dogs to trample but I have no energy for extra heartbreak, this month last year the month of my sister's diagnosis and her gone before winter solstice. But I shouldn't forget the compost pile, all the vegetable detritus and tea bags and egg cartons mixing into a rank stew, the miracle of carbon breaking down so in a few months I can remove the lower panel and shovel out something better, richer, the result of neglect and transformation in the dark.

Oh, believe me, I know, the shadows of leaves sway and flutter over the grass, a hundred hands waving, and every time I breathe, I am waving back.

Auditory Pareidolia

I hear voices in the bathroom fan and sometimes the dish-washer, but I cannot make out what they're saying. Perhaps a group of people have suddenly arrived in my house, chat loudly in the hall. Perhaps my husband shouts from the bedroom, frantic. I wish I could hear my sister speak again, her voice so like mine, even the last time she said anything that made sense, calling out our niece's nickname as she approached the hospital bed in the living room to say good-bye for the last time. There was joy in that greeting, and hearing it ruined me. I turned to the dog, whispered his name, sank my fingers into his white fur. He seemed to be the only one who would miss her as much as I did.

It is summer now, and the neighbors' kids scream from backyard pools. No one calls out, in need, from another room. Humans seek patterns: that's why we hear voices in white noise, see faces in the clouds. If only I could stand in the shower, the fan mixing up its conversations just for me, until I hear her say *It's wonderful here.* The universe is full of things that haven't even been named yet. It could happen.

ACKNOWLEDGMENTS

Grateful acknowledgment to the editors of the following publications where these pieces appeared, sometimes in different forms.

Buddhist Poetry Review—"Mind Like the Sky"
Carve—"The Country of After-Grief"
One—"Dear Night Skies of the 1970s"
One Art—"She Wanted to Go to the Sea One Last Time"
Phi Kappa Phi Forum—"Prey"
Sky Island Journal—"Grief Uninvented"
Spoon River Poetry Review—"What You Deserve"
SWWIM—"Ordering a Zero Gravity Chair Online"
Vox Viola—"Astronomy"

Special thanks to Carolyn Alessio, a brilliant writer and my best friend from college who still supports me emotionally and editorially after all these years; writer friend Christine Lasek, who gave me much-needed permission to think of this book as a collage; Lisa Lanser Rose and The Gloria Sirens, who supported me simply by asking what I was writing, week after week; Dr. Ross Tangedal, publisher of Cornerstone Press, for his belief in this book and his patience; the student and faculty team at Cornerstone Press for so much hard work designing and promoting; and most of all, my husband, Andy, whose steady kindness and dad-joke humor buoys me every day.

KATHERINE RIEGEL is the author of the poetry books *Love Songs from the End of the World* (2019), *What the Mouth Was Made For* (2013), and *Castaway* (2010); her prose poetry/creative nonfiction chapbook *Letters to Colin Firth* won the Sundress Press chapbook competition in 2015. Her work has appeared in *Brevity, Cream City Review, The Gettysburg Review, The Offing, One, Orion, Poets.org, SWWIM, Tin House*, and many other literary publications. After receiving an MFA in poetry from the Iowa Writers Workshop, she taught writing at various colleges and universities for almost 25 years, most recently the University of South Florida. She is co-founder and managing editor of the literary magazine *Sweet* and teaches online classes in poetry and creative nonfiction.